MASTER INDEX &
SHOP MANUAL

Other Publications:

AMERICAN COUNTRY

VOYAGE THROUGH THE UNIVERSE

THE THIRD REICH

THE TIME-LIFE GARDENER'S GUIDE

MYSTERIES OF THE UNKNOWN

TIME FRAME

FIX IT YOURSELF

FITNESS, HEALTH & NUTRITION

SUCCESSFUL PARENTING

HEALTHY HOME COOKING

UNDERSTANDING COMPUTERS

LIBRARY OF NATIONS

THE ENCHANTED WORLD

THE KODAK LIBRARY OF CREATIVE PHOTOGRAPHY

GREAT MEALS IN MINUTES

THE CIVIL WAR

PLANET EARTH

COLLECTOR'S LIBRARY OF THE CIVIL WAR

THE EPIC OF FLIGHT

THE GOOD COOK

WORLD WAR II

HOME REPAIR AND IMPROVEMENT

THE OLD WEST

MASTER INDEX & SHOP MANUAL

TIME-LIFE BOOKS
ALEXANDRIA, VIRGINIA

Fix It Yourself was produced by
ST. REMY PRESS

MANAGING EDITOR	Kenneth Winchester
MANAGING ART DIRECTOR	Pierre Léveillé

Staff for *Master Index & Shop Manual*

Series Editor	Brian Parsons
Editor	Marc Cassini
Series Art Director	Diane Denoncourt
Art Director	Solange Laberge
Research Editor	Naomi Fukuyama
Designers	Chantal Bilodeau, Luc Germain, Julie Léger
Contributing Writer	Grant Loewen
Contributing Illustrators	Gérard Mariscalchi, Jacques Proulx
Cover	Robert Monté
Master index	Christine M. Jacobs, Christina Richards
Administrator	Natalie Watanabe
Production Manager	Michelle Turbide
Coordinator	Dominique Gagné
Systems Coordinator	Jean-Luc Roy
Photographer	Robert Chartier

Time-Life Books Inc. is a wholly owned subsidiary of
THE TIME INC. BOOK COMPANY

President and Chief Executive Officer	Kelso F. Sutton
President, Time Inc. Books Direct	Christopher T. Linen

TIME-LIFE BOOKS INC.

Managing Editor	Thomas H. Flaherty
Director of Editorial Resources	Elise D. Ritter-Clough
Director of Photography and Research	John Conrad Weiser
Editorial Board	Dale Brown, Roberta Conlan, Laura Foreman, Lee Hassig, Jim Hicks, Blaine Marshall, Rita Mullin, Henry Woodhead
PUBLISHER	Joseph J. Ward
Associate Publisher	Trevor Lunn
Editorial Director	Donia Steele
Marketing Director	Regina Hall
Director of Design	Louis Klein
Production Manager	Marlene Zack
Supervisor of Quality Control	James King

Editorial Operations

Production	Celia Beattie
Library	Louise D. Forstall
Correspondents	Elisabeth Kraemer-Singh (Bonn); Christina Lieberman (New York); Maria Vincenza Aloisi (Paris); Ann Natanson (Rome).

THE CONSULTANTS

Richard Day, a do-it-yourself writer for nearly a quarter of a century, is a founder of the National Association of Home and Workshop Writers and is the author of several repair books.

Kathleen M. Kiely was a Series Editor of *Fix It Yourself*. She has worked as a writer and editor for other Time-Life Books series, including *Home Repair and Improvement*, *Your Home* and *Planet Earth*.

Library of Congress Cataloging-in-Publication Data
Master index & shop manual
    p. cm. – (Fix it yourself)
    ISBN 0-8094-7330-1 (trade).
    ISBN 0-8094-7331-X (lib.).
    1. Fix it yourself—Indexes. 2. Dwellings—Maintenance and repair—Amateurs' manuals. 3. Dwellings—Maintenance and repair—Indexes.
    I. Time-Life Books. II. Title: Master index and shop manual III. Series.
    TH4817.I54 1991
    643'. 7—dc20   90-26067
                                CIP

For information about any Time-Life book, please write:
Reader Information
Time-Life Customer Service
P.O. Box C-32068
Richmond, Virginia
23261-2068

CONTENTS

HOW TO USE THIS BOOK

Master Index & Shop Manual is a comprehensive reference guide to the volumes of the Fix It Yourself series. Shown below are four sample pages from the book, one page from each section, with captions describing the various features and how they work.

The Master Index—the heart of the book—is a complete index of the Fix It Yourself series, providing subject references to all the repairs, tools and techniques, and emergency procedures presented in every volume. For each subject reference, there is a list of the relevant volumes of the Fix It Yourself series, with page

numbers coded to indicate Troubleshooting Guides and sections on repairs, tools and techniques, and emergency procedures. For example, if your problem is damaged carpeting, page 12 of the Master Index will refer you to a number of volumes for specific types of information: *Cleaning & Stain Removal*, *Fixing Your House To Sell* and *Floors, Stairs & Carpets*, for instance. Or, if you are seeking information on the tools and techniques for using carriage bolts, you will be referred to specific pages in *Home Workshop Techniques*.

Emergency procedures
Page references printed in red indicate emergency procedures on the subject mentioned.

Repair procedures
Page references for step-by-step repair procedures on the subject mentioned are printed in black; bold type is used to indicate Troubleshooting Guides.

Section headings
From the table of contents, you will be referred directly to the first page of each section on specific materials and supplies or tools and safety equipment.

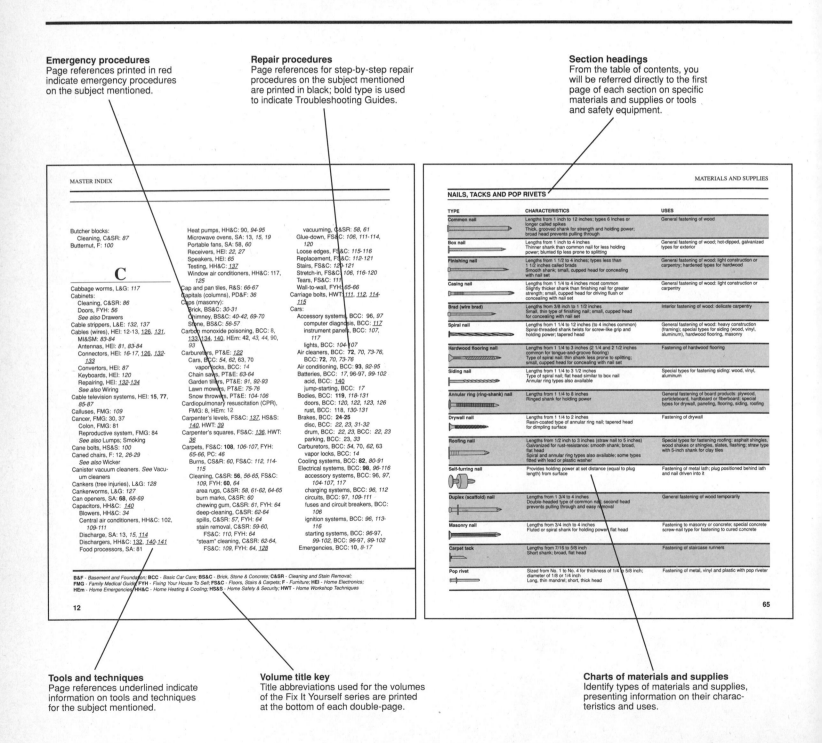

Tools and techniques
Page references underlined indicate information on tools and techniques for the subject mentioned.

Volume title key
Title abbreviations used for the volumes of the Fix It Yourself series are printed at the bottom of each double-page.

Charts of materials and supplies
Identify types of materials and supplies, presenting information on their characteristics and uses.

The shop-manual sections entitled Materials and Supplies and Tools and Safety Equipment are designed for handy reference to the wide range of materials, supplies, tools and safety equipment used in home repairs. Materials and Supplies lists information ranging from standard sizes of lumber, sheet metal and fasteners to types of pipe fittings, electrical wires and cables, cleaning agents and pesticides. Tools and Safety Equipment presents the basic home repair kit of tools and safety equipment, including information on their features, accessories and uses. Refer to these sections for guidance in gathering together the materials and tools you need for a repair job.

The final section is the Glossary, a selective listing of explanations for key terms, phrases, abbreviations and acronyns common to home repairs. Included are charts for simple converting between U.S. and metric standard units, as well as between Fahrenheit and Celsius temperatures. Also presented are illustrated inventories of common wood cuts, wood joints, chemical product safety symbols and electronic safety symbols.

Variations
Differences in tools and safety equipment are highlighted.

Abbreviations
Provide the meaning of common acronyms specific to home repairs.

Definitions
Explain key terms and phrases specific to home repairs.

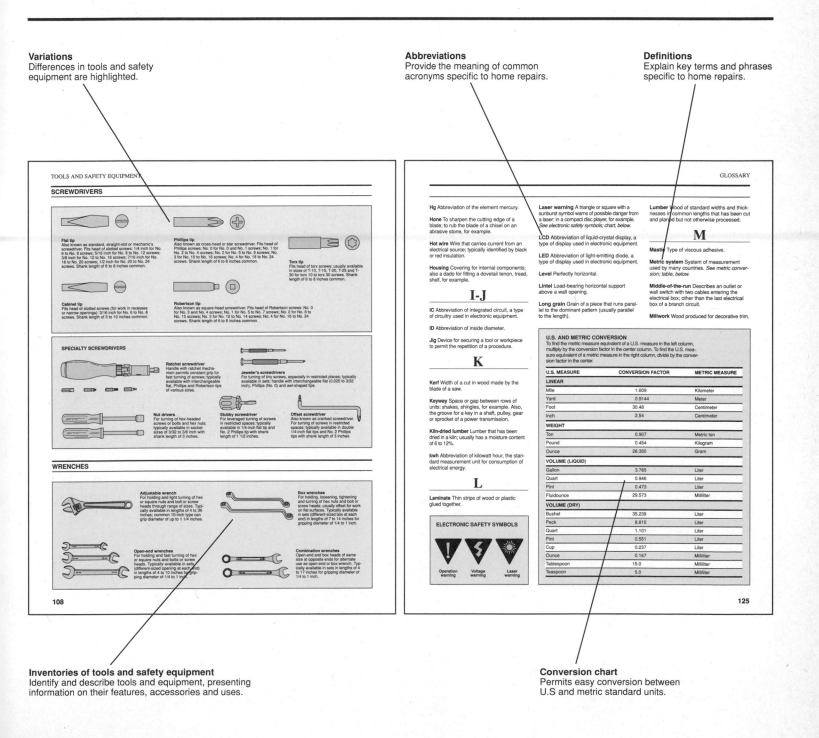

Inventories of tools and safety equipment
Identify and describe tools and equipment, presenting information on their features, accessories and uses.

Conversion chart
Permits easy conversion between U.S and metric standard units.

MASTER INDEX

B&F - *Basement and Foundation;* **BCC** - *Basic Car Care;* **BS&C** - *Brick, Stone & Concrete;* **C&SR** - *Cleaning and Stain Removal;*
FMG - *Family Medical Guide;* **FYH** - *Fixing Your House To Sell;* **FS&C** - *Floors, Stairs & Carpets;* **F** - *Furniture;* **HEI** - *Home Electronics;*
HEm - *Home Emergencies;* **HH&C** - *Home Heating & Cooling;* **HS&S** - *Home Safety & Security;* **HWT** - *Home Workshop Techniques*

8

B

K&BP - *Kitchen & Bathroom Plumbing;* **L&G** - *Lawn & Garden;* **L&E** - *Lighting & Electricity;* **MA** - *Major Appliances;* **OH** - *The Older House;* **PC** - *Pest Control;* **PD&F** - *Porches, Decks & Fences;* **PT&E** - *Power Tools & Equipment;* **R&S** - *Roofing & Siding;* **SA** - *Small Appliances;* **WC&W** - *Walls, Ceilings & Woodwork;* **W&D** - *Windows & Doors;* **MI&SM** - *Master Index & Shop Manual*

B&F - *Basement and Foundation;* **BCC** - *Basic Car Care;* **BS&C** - *Brick, Stone & Concrete;* **C&SR** - *Cleaning and Stain Removal;*
FMG - *Family Medical Guide;* **FYH** - *Fixing Your House To Sell;* **FS&C** - *Floors, Stairs & Carpets;* **F** - *Furniture;* **HEI** - *Home Electronics;*
HEm - *Home Emergencies;* **HH&C** - *Home Heating & Cooling;* **HS&S** - *Home Safety & Security;* **HWT** - *Home Workshop Techniques*

10

K&BP - *Kitchen & Bathroom Plumbing;* **L&G** - *Lawn & Garden;* **L&E** - *Lighting & Electricity;* **MA** - *Major Appliances;* **OH** - *The Older House;*
PC - *Pest Control;* **PD&F** - *Porches, Decks & Fences;* **PT&E** - *Power Tools & Equipment;* **R&S** - *Roofing & Siding;* **SA** - *Small Appliances;*
WC&W - *Walls, Ceilings & Woodwork;* **W&D** - *Windows & Doors;* **MI&SM** - *Master Index & Shop Manual*

11

B&F - *Basement and Foundation;* **BCC** - *Basic Car Care;* **BS&C** - *Brick, Stone & Concrete;* **C&SR** - *Cleaning and Stain Removal;*
FMG - *Family Medical Guide;* **FYH** - *Fixing Your House To Sell;* **FS&C** - *Floors, Stairs & Carpets;* **F** - *Furniture;* **HEI** - *Home Electronics;*
HEm - *Home Emergencies;* **HH&C** - *Home Heating & Cooling;* **HS&S** - *Home Safety & Security;* **HWT** - *Home Workshop Techniques*

K&BP - *Kitchen & Bathroom Plumbing;* **L&G** - *Lawn & Garden;* **L&E** - *Lighting & Electricity;* **MA** - *Major Appliances;* **OH** - *The Older House;*
PC - *Pest Control;* **PD&F** - *Porches, Decks & Fences;* **PT&E** - *Power Tools & Equipment;* **R&S** - *Roofing & Siding;* **SA** - *Small Appliances;*
WC&W - *Walls, Ceilings & Woodwork;* **W&D** - *Windows & Doors;* **MI&SM** - *Master Index & Shop Manual*

B&F - *Basement and Foundation;* **BCC** - *Basic Car Care;* **BS&C** - *Brick, Stone & Concrete;* **C&SR** - *Cleaning and Stain Removal;*
FMG - *Family Medical Guide;* **FYH** - *Fixing Your House To Sell;* **FS&C** - *Floors, Stairs & Carpets;* **F** - *Furniture;* **HEI** - *Home Electronics;*
HEm - *Home Emergencies;* **HH&C** - *Home Heating & Cooling;* **HS&S** - *Home Safety & Security;* **HWT** - *Home Workshop Techniques*

14

B&F - *Basement and Foundation;* **BCC** - *Basic Car Care;* **BS&C** - *Brick, Stone & Concrete;* **C&SR** - *Cleaning and Stain Removal;*
FMG - *Family Medical Guide;* **FYH** - *Fixing Your House To Sell;* **FS&C** - *Floors, Stairs & Carpets;* **F** - *Furniture;* **HEI** - *Home Electronics;*
HEm - *Home Emergencies;* **HH&C** - *Home Heating & Cooling;* **HS&S** - *Home Safety & Security;* **HWT** - *Home Workshop Techniques*

K&BP - *Kitchen & Bathroom Plumbing;* **L&G** - *Lawn & Garden;* **L&E** - *Lighting & Electricity;* **MA** - *Major Appliances;* **OH** - *The Older House;*
PC - *Pest Control;* **PD&F** - *Porches, Decks & Fences;* **PT&E** - *Power Tools & Equipment;* **R&S** - *Roofing & Siding;* **SA** - *Small Appliances;*
WC&W - *Walls, Ceilings & Woodwork;* **W&D** - *Windows & Doors;* **MI&SM** - *Master Index & Shop Manual*

D

K&BP - _Kitchen & Bathroom Plumbing;_ **L&G** - _Lawn & Garden;_ **L&E** - _Lighting & Electricity;_ **MA** - _Major Appliances;_ **OH** - _The Older House;_
PC - _Pest Control;_ **PD&F** - _Porches, Decks & Fences;_ **PT&E** - _Power Tools & Equipment;_ **R&S** - _Roofing & Siding;_ **SA** - _Small Appliances;_
WC&W - _Walls, Ceilings & Woodwork;_ **W&D** - _Windows & Doors;_ **MI&SM** - _Master Index & Shop Manual_

K&BP - *Kitchen & Bathroom Plumbing;* **L&G** - *Lawn & Garden;* **L&E** - *Lighting & Electricity;* **MA** - *Major Appliances;* **OH** - *The Older House;*
PC - *Pest Control;* **PD&F** - *Porches, Decks & Fences;* **PT&E** - *Power Tools & Equipment;* **R&S** - *Roofing & Siding;* **SA** - *Small Appliances;*
WC&W - *Walls, Ceilings & Woodwork;* **W&D** - *Windows & Doors;* **MI&SM** - *Master Index & Shop Manual*

B&F - *Basement and Foundation;* **BCC** - *Basic Car Care;* **BS&C** - *Brick, Stone & Concrete;* **C&SR** - *Cleaning and Stain Removal;*
FMG - *Family Medical Guide;* **FYH** - *Fixing Your House To Sell;* **FS&C** - *Floors, Stairs & Carpets;* **F** - *Furniture;* **HEI** - *Home Electronics;*
HEm - *Home Emergencies;* **HH&C** - *Home Heating & Cooling;* **HS&S** - *Home Safety & Security;* **HWT** - *Home Workshop Techniques*

22

F

B&F - *Basement and Foundation;* **BCC** - *Basic Car Care;* **BS&C** - *Brick, Stone & Concrete;* **C&SR** - *Cleaning and Stain Removal;*
FMG - *Family Medical Guide;* **FYH** - *Fixing Your House To Sell;* **FS&C** - *Floors, Stairs & Carpets;* **F** - *Furniture;* **HEl** - *Home Electronics;*
HEm - *Home Emergencies;* **HH&C** - *Home Heating & Cooling;* **HS&S** - *Home Safety & Security;* **HWT** - *Home Workshop Techniques*

K&BP - *Kitchen & Bathroom Plumbing;* **L&G** - *Lawn & Garden;* **L&E** - *Lighting & Electricity;* **MA** - *Major Appliances;* **OH** - *The Older House;*
PC - *Pest Control;* **PD&F** - *Porches, Decks & Fences;* **PT&E** - *Power Tools & Equipment;* **R&S** - *Roofing & Siding;* **SA** - *Small Appliances;*
WC&W - *Walls, Ceilings & Woodwork;* **W&D** - *Windows & Doors;* **MI&SM** - *Master Index & Shop Manual*

Frostbite, FMG: **11**, **102**, 26, 100, 107, HEm: *36*
Frozen pipes, HEm: 96, *101*
Fruit canes, L&G: *47*
Fuel, PT&E: 8
  Drainage, PT&E: *124*
  Mixing with oil, PT&E: *121*
  Refueling, PT&E: 8, *121*
  Spills, PT&E: *11*
  See also Gas; Gasoline; Oil
Fuel filters:
  Chain saws, PT&E: *64-65*
  Lawn mowers, PT&E: *74*
  Snow throwers, PT&E: *107*
  String trimmers, PT&E: *53*
Fuel injection, BCC: *55*, *62-63*
Fuel systems:
  Cars, BCC: **64**, 54, *62-69*
    filters, BCC: 63, *65-66*
    pumps, BCC: 63, *66-67*
Fungal leaf spots, L&G: *120*
Fungicides. *See* Pesticides
Furnaces:
  Cleaning, FYH: *121*
  Filters, CS&R: *107-108*, FYH: *122*
  High-efficiency gas, HH&C: 68
  Humidifiers, FYH: *123*
  See also Air distribution systems;
    Electric furnaces; Gas burners;
    Oil burners; Thermostats
Furniture:
  Cleaning, C&SR: **66**, *67-77*
    laminates, C&SR: *73*
    plastics, C&SR: *71*
    wicker, C&SR: *71*
    wood, C&SR: *73-76*
  Salvage, HEm: *139*, *140*
  Surface repairs, F: **84**-*85*
    burns, F: *91*
    cracks, F: *89-90*
    dents, F: *91*
    marble, F: *95*
    plastic laminates, F: *93*, *95*
    scratches, F: *88*
    veneers, F: *93-95*

Upholstery fires, HEm: *62*
See also Outdoor furniture; Refin-
  ishing: Furniture; Upholstered fur-
  niture; names of specific types of
  furniture
Furring strips, R&S: *100*
Fusarium:
  Blight, L&G: *124*
  Wilt, L&G: *114*
Fuses, HEm: *82*, *83*, *84*, *86*, HH&C:
  134, HS&S: 20, 22, HWT: *10*, L&E:
  15, 16, *18-19*, MA: *132*, OH: *104*,
  PT&E: *112*, WC&W: *137*, MI&SM:
  82
  Alarm controls, HS&S: *127*
  Blenders, SA: *79*
  Cars, BCC: *106*
  Clothes dryer, MA: 114-115, *120*
  Coffee makers, SA: *43*
  Electric furnaces, HH&C: *80*
  Electric ranges, MA: 42, *54*
  Electronic stand mixers, SA: *77*
  Home electronics, HEI: *128*, *137*
    monitors, HEI: *118*
    printers, HEI: *124*
    receivers, HEI: *23*, *26*
    televisions, HEI: *72*
    videocassette recorders, HEI: *95*,
      97
  Microwave ovens, SA: *16*
  Toaster ovens, SA: *30*
  See also Circuit breakers; Service
    panels

G

Gables:
  Vents, R&S: *23*
Galvanized steel pipes, K&BP: 93
  Dimensions, K&BP: *95*
  Repairs, HEm: *103-104*, K&BP: *101*,
    OH: *94*, *97-99*
    with copper pipes, K&BP: *102*

with CPVC pipes, K&BP: *104-
  105*
with PB pipes, K&BP: *103*
Garage doors, FYH: *81*, HS&S: *99-
  100*, PC: *24*, W&D: **103**, *102-107*
  Alarm systems, HS&S: *113*
  Automatic openers, W&D: *102*, 103,
    104
  Safety precautions, W&D: 8, 103,
    104
  Weather stripping, W&D: *103*
Garages:
  Cleaning, FYH: 86, *88*
  Home, BCC: *134*
  Moisture, FYH: 86, *89-90*
  Professional, BCC: *136*
  See also Garage doors; Profession-
    al services: Cars
Garbage can stands, PC: *71-72*
Garbage disposers, K&BP: *38*, *42*, *45*,
  MA: **87**, *86-87*
  Access, MA: *88*
  Clogs, MA: 86-87, *89*
  Flywheels, MA: *90-91*
  Shredder rings, MA: *90-91*
  Switches, MA: *89-90*, MA: *89-91*
Garden frost, L&G: *13*
Gardens, FYH: *22-23*, L&G: **33-34**, *32-
  47*, *14-15*
  Pests, PC: **76-77**, *74-75*
    barriers, PC: *88*, *96*, *97*
    foliage, PC: *84*, *86*, *87-89*
    identification, PC: *78-81*
    soil, PC: *84*, *87*, *88*, *89*
    trees, PC: *90*, *95-97*
  See also Lawns; Pesticides; Plants;
    Soil
Garden tillers, PT&E: *85*, *84*, *86*, L&G:
  132
  Air filters, PT&E: *87*
  Carburetors, PT&E: *91*, *92-93*
  Cooling fins, PT&E: *93*
  Drive belts, PT&E: *89*
  Electronic ignition modules, PT&E:
    95

B&F - *Basement and Foundation;* **BCC** - *Basic Car Care;* **BS&C** - *Brick, Stone & Concrete;* **C&SR** - *Cleaning and Stain Removal;*
FMG - *Family Medical Guide;* **FYH** - *Fixing Your House To Sell;* **FS&C** - *Floors, Stairs & Carpets;* **F** - *Furniture;* **HEI** - *Home Electronics;*
HEm - *Home Emergencies;* **HH&C** - *Home Heating & Cooling;* **HS&S** - *Home Safety & Security;* **HWT** - *Home Workshop Techniques*

K&BP - *Kitchen & Bathroom Plumbing;* **L&G** - *Lawn & Garden;* **L&E** - *Lighting & Electricity;* **MA** - *Major Appliances;* **OH** - *The Older House;*
PC - *Pest Control;* **PD&F** - *Porches, Decks & Fences;* **PT&E** - *Power Tools & Equipment;* **R&S** - *Roofing & Siding;* **SA** - *Small Appliances;*
WC&W - *Walls, Ceilings & Woodwork;* **W&D** - *Windows & Doors;* **MI&SM** - *Master Index & Shop Manual*

B&F - *Basement and Foundation;* **BCC** - *Basic Car Care;* **BS&C** - *Brick, Stone & Concrete;* **C&SR** - *Cleaning and Stain Removal;*
FMG - *Family Medical Guide;* **FYH** - *Fixing Your House To Sell;* **FS&C** - *Floors, Stairs & Carpets;* **F** - *Furniture;* **HEI** - *Home Electronics;*
HEm - *Home Emergencies;* **HH&C** - *Home Heating & Cooling;* **HS&S** - *Home Safety & Security;* **HWT** - *Home Workshop Techniques*

28

I

K&BP - *Kitchen & Bathroom Plumbing;* **L&G** - *Lawn & Garden;* **L&E** - *Lighting & Electricity;* **MA** - *Major Appliances;* **OH** - *The Older House;*
PC - *Pest Control;* **PD&F** - *Porches, Decks & Fences;* **PT&E** - *Power Tools & Equipment;* **R&S** - *Roofing & Siding;* **SA** - *Small Appliances;*
WC&W - *Walls, Ceilings & Woodwork;* **W&D** - *Windows & Doors;* **MI&SM** - *Master Index & Shop Manual*

29

M

B&F - *Basement and Foundation;* **BCC** - *Basic Car Care;* **BS&C** - *Brick, Stone & Concrete;* **C&SR** - *Cleaning and Stain Removal;*
FMG - *Family Medical Guide;* **FYH** - *Fixing Your House To Sell;* **FS&C** - *Floors, Stairs & Carpets;* **F** - *Furniture;* **HEI** - *Home Electronics;*
HEm - *Home Emergencies;* **HH&C** - *Home Heating & Cooling;* **HS&S** - *Home Safety & Security;* **HWT** - *Home Workshop Techniques*

K&BP - *Kitchen & Bathroom Plumbing;* **L&G** - *Lawn & Garden;* **L&E** - *Lighting & Electricity;* **MA** - *Major Appliances;* **OH** - *The Older House;*
PC - *Pest Control;* **PD&F** - *Porches, Decks & Fences;* **PT&E** - *Power Tools & Equipment;* **R&S** - *Roofing & Siding;* **SA** - *Small Appliances;*
WC&W - *Walls, Ceilings & Woodwork;* **W&D** - *Windows & Doors;* **MI&SM** - *Master Index & Shop Manual*

N

O

B&F - *Basement and Foundation;* **BCC** - *Basic Car Care;* **BS&C** - *Brick, Stone & Concrete;* **C&SR** - *Cleaning and Stain Removal;*
FMG - *Family Medical Guide;* **FYH** - *Fixing Your House To Sell;* **FS&C** - *Floors, Stairs & Carpets;* **F** - *Furniture;* **HEI** - *Home Electronics;*
HEm - *Home Emergencies;* **HH&C** - *Home Heating & Cooling;* **HS&S** - *Home Safety & Security;* **HWT** - *Home Workshop Techniques*

K&BP - *Kitchen & Bathroom Plumbing;* **L&G** - *Lawn & Garden;* **L&E** - *Lighting & Electricity;* **MA** - *Major Appliances;* **OH** - *The Older House;*
PC - *Pest Control;* **PD&F** - *Porches, Decks & Fences;* **PT&E** - *Power Tools & Equipment;* **R&S** - *Roofing & Siding;* **SA** - *Small Appliances;*
WC&W - *Walls, Ceilings & Woodwork;* **W&D** - *Windows & Doors;* **MI&SM** - *Master Index & Shop Manual*

K&BP - *Kitchen & Bathroom Plumbing;* **L&G** - *Lawn & Garden;* **L&E** - *Lighting & Electricity;* **MA** - *Major Appliances;* **OH** - *The Older House;*
PC - *Pest Control;* **PD&F** - *Porches, Decks & Fences;* **PT&E** - *Power Tools & Equipment;* **R&S** - *Roofing & Siding;* **SA** - *Small Appliances;*
WC&W - *Walls, Ceilings & Woodwork;* **W&D** - *Windows & Doors;* **MI&SM** - *Master Index & Shop Manual*

B&F - *Basement and Foundation;* **BCC** - *Basic Car Care;* **BS&C** - *Brick, Stone & Concrete;* **C&SR** - *Cleaning and Stain Removal;*
FMG - *Family Medical Guide;* **FYH** - *Fixing Your House To Sell;* **FS&C** - *Floors, Stairs & Carpets;* **F** - *Furniture;* **HEI** - *Home Electronics;*
HEm - *Home Emergencies;* **HH&C** - *Home Heating & Cooling;* **HS&S** - *Home Safety & Security;* **HWT** - *Home Workshop Techniques*

38

K&BP - *Kitchen & Bathroom Plumbing;* **L&G** - *Lawn & Garden;* **L&E** - *Lighting & Electricity;* **MA** - *Major Appliances;* **OH** - *The Older House;*
PC - *Pest Control;* **PD&F** - *Porches, Decks & Fences;* **PT&E** - *Power Tools & Equipment;* **R&S** - *Roofing & Siding;* **SA** - *Small Appliances;*
WC&W - *Walls, Ceilings & Woodwork;* **W&D** - *Windows & Doors;* **MI&SM** - *Master Index & Shop Manual*

S

K&BP - *Kitchen & Bathroom Plumbing;* **L&G** - *Lawn & Garden;* **L&E** - *Lighting & Electricity;* **MA** - *Major Appliances;* **OH** - *The Older House;*
PC - *Pest Control;* **PD&F** - *Porches, Decks & Fences;* **PT&E** - *Power Tools & Equipment;* **R&S** - *Roofing & Siding;* **SA** - *Small Appliances;*
WC&W - *Walls, Ceilings & Woodwork;* **W&D** - *Windows & Doors;* **MI&SM** - *Master Index & Shop Manual*

B&F - *Basement and Foundation;* **BCC** - *Basic Car Care;* **BS&C** - *Brick, Stone & Concrete;* **C&SR** - *Cleaning and Stain Removal;*
FMG - *Family Medical Guide;* **FYH** - *Fixing Your House To Sell;* **FS&C** - *Floors, Stairs & Carpets;* **F** - *Furniture;* **HEl** - *Home Electronics;*
HEm - *Home Emergencies;* **HH&C** - *Home Heating & Cooling;* **HS&S** - *Home Safety & Security;* **HWT** - *Home Workshop Techniques*

K&BP - _Kitchen & Bathroom Plumbing;_ **L&G** - _Lawn & Garden;_ **L&E** - _Lighting & Electricity;_ **MA** - _Major Appliances;_ **OH** - _The Older House;_
PC - _Pest Control;_ **PD&F** - _Porches, Decks & Fences;_ **PT&E** - _Power Tools & Equipment;_ **R&S** - _Roofing & Siding;_ **SA** - _Small Appliances;_
WC&W - _Walls, Ceilings & Woodwork;_ **W&D** - _Windows & Doors;_ **MI&SM** - _Master Index & Shop Manual_

B&F - *Basement and Foundation;* **BCC** - *Basic Car Care;* **BS&C** - *Brick, Stone & Concrete;* **C&SR** - *Cleaning and Stain Removal;*
FMG - *Family Medical Guide;* **FYH** - *Fixing Your House To Sell;* **FS&C** - *Floors, Stairs & Carpets;* **F** - *Furniture;* **HEI** - *Home Electronics;*
HEm - *Home Emergencies;* **HH&C** - *Home Heating & Cooling;* **HS&S** - *Home Safety & Security;* **HWT** - *Home Workshop Techniques*

B&F - *Basement and Foundation;* **BCC** - *Basic Car Care;* **BS&C** - *Brick, Stone & Concrete;* **C&SR** - *Cleaning and Stain Removal;*
FMG - *Family Medical Guide;* **FYH** - *Fixing Your House To Sell;* **FS&C** - *Floors, Stairs & Carpets;* **F** - *Furniture;* **HEI** - *Home Electronics;*
HEm - *Home Emergencies;* **HH&C** - *Home Heating & Cooling;* **HS&S** - *Home Safety & Security;* **HWT** - *Home Workshop Techniques*

T

K&BP - *Kitchen & Bathroom Plumbing;* **L&G** - *Lawn & Garden;* **L&E** - *Lighting & Electricity;* **MA** - *Major Appliances;* **OH** - *The Older House;*
PC - *Pest Control;* **PD&F** - *Porches, Decks & Fences;* **PT&E** - *Power Tools & Equipment;* **R&S** - *Roofing & Siding;* **SA** - *Small Appliances;*
WC&W - *Walls, Ceilings & Woodwork;* **W&D** - *Windows & Doors;* **MI&SM** - *Master Index & Shop Manual*

B&F - *Basement and Foundation;* **BCC** - *Basic Car Care;* **BS&C** - *Brick, Stone & Concrete;* **C&SR** - *Cleaning and Stain Removal;*
FMG - *Family Medical Guide;* **FYH** - *Fixing Your House To Sell;* **FS&C** - *Floors, Stairs & Carpets;* **F** - *Furniture;* **HEI** - *Home Electronics;*
HEm - *Home Emergencies;* **HH&C** - *Home Heating & Cooling;* **HS&S** - *Home Safety & Security;* **HWT** - *Home Workshop Techniques*

K&BP - *Kitchen & Bathroom Plumbing;* **L&G** - *Lawn & Garden;* **L&E** - *Lighting & Electricity;* **MA** - *Major Appliances;* **OH** - *The Older House;*
PC - *Pest Control;* **PD&F** - *Porches, Decks & Fences;* **PT&E** - *Power Tools & Equipment;* **R&S** - *Roofing & Siding;* **SA** - *Small Appliances;*
WC&W - *Walls, Ceilings & Woodwork;* **W&D** - *Windows & Doors;* **MI&SM** - *Master Index & Shop Manual*

B&F - *Basement and Foundation;* **BCC** - *Basic Car Care;* **BS&C** - *Brick, Stone & Concrete;* **C&SR** - *Cleaning and Stain Removal;*
FMG - *Family Medical Guide;* **FYH** - *Fixing Your House To Sell;* **FS&C** - *Floors, Stairs & Carpets;* **F** - *Furniture;* **HEI** - *Home Electronics;*
HEm - *Home Emergencies;* **HH&C** - *Home Heating & Cooling;* **HS&S** - *Home Safety & Security;* **HWT** - *Home Workshop Techniques*

K&BP - *Kitchen & Bathroom Plumbing;* **L&G** - *Lawn & Garden;* **L&E** - *Lighting & Electricity;* **MA** - *Major Appliances;* **OH** - *The Older House;*
PC - *Pest Control;* **PD&F** - *Porches, Decks & Fences;* **PT&E** - *Power Tools & Equipment;* **R&S** - *Roofing & Siding;* **SA** - *Small Appliances;*
WC&W - *Walls, Ceilings & Woodwork;* **W&D** - *Windows & Doors;* **MI&SM** - *Master Index & Shop Manual*

53

B&F - *Basement and Foundation;* **BCC** - *Basic Car Care;* **BS&C** - *Brick, Stone & Concrete;* **C&SR** - *Cleaning and Stain Removal;*
FMG - *Family Medical Guide;* **FYH** - *Fixing Your House To Sell;* **FS&C** - *Floors, Stairs & Carpets;* **F** - *Furniture;* **HE!** - *Home Electronics;*
HEm - *Home Emergencies;* **HH&C** - *Home Heating & Cooling;* **HS&S** - *Home Safety & Security;* **HWT** - *Home Workshop Techniques*

54

K&BP - *Kitchen & Bathroom Plumbing;* **L&G** - *Lawn & Garden;* **L&E** - *Lighting & Electricity;* **MA** - *Major Appliances;* **OH** - *The Older House;*
PC - *Pest Control;* **PD&F** - *Porches, Decks & Fences;* **PT&E** - *Power Tools & Equipment;* **R&S** - *Roofing & Siding;* **SA** - *Small Appliances;*
WC&W - *Walls, Ceilings & Woodwork;* **W&D** - *Windows & Doors;* **MI&SM** - *Master Index & Shop Manual*

B&F - *Basement and Foundation;* **BCC** - *Basic Car Care;* **BS&C** - *Brick, Stone & Concrete;* **C&SR** - *Cleaning and Stain Removal;*
FMG - *Family Medical Guide;* **FYH** - *Fixing Your House To Sell;* **FS&C** - *Floors, Stairs & Carpets;* **F** - *Furniture;* **HEI** - *Home Electronics;*
HEm - *Home Emergencies;* **HH&C** - *Home Heating & Cooling;* **HS&S** - *Home Safety & Security;* **HWT** - *Home Workshop Techniques*

Y

K&BP - *Kitchen & Bathroom Plumbing;* **L&G** - *Lawn & Garden;* **L&E** - *Lighting & Electricity;* **MA** - *Major Appliances;* **OH** - *The Older House;*
PC - *Pest Control;* **PD&F** - *Porches, Decks & Fences;* **PT&E** - *Power Tools & Equipment;* **R&S** - *Roofing & Siding;* **SA** - *Small Appliances;*
WC&W - *Walls, Ceilings & Woodwork;* **W&D** - *Windows & Doors;* **MI&SM** - *Master Index & Shop Manual*

MATERIALS AND SUPPLIES

LUMBER

TYPE	CHARACTERISTICS	USES
SOFTWOOD		
Cedar	Red-brown to pale yellow; fine, straight grain Relatively weak, but high resistance to decay: western types light and soft; eastern types heavy and hard Easy to shape; hold on fasteners poor; glue and paint bond well	Exterior siding (shingles, shakes, clapboards); fences; decks; closets (lining)
Fir	Red-brown to pale cream; fine, straight grain Exceptionally strong, but tends to split when exposed to weather; light to heavy and fairly soft Easy to shape, but tends to tear; hold on fasteners average; paint bonds poorly	Load-bearing framing (girders, joists, studs); some types suitable for interior trim
Hemlock	Pale brown and semi-lustrous; straight grain Eastern types relatively weak; western types relatively strong: tends to split; light and fairly hard Easy to shape; hold on fasteners poor; paint bonds poorly	Rough framing (studs); interior trim
Larch	Pale to rich red; straight grain with many small knots Strong and rigid, but high shrinkage; heavy and fairly hard Hard to shape, tending to splinter and tear; hold on fasteners good, but often splits when nailed; paint bonds well	Rough framing (studs); not suitable for interior trim
Pine	White to pale or red-brown, often with streaks of red; fine to fairly coarse, straight grain Strong; low shrinkage and warpage when dried, but tends to split when exposed to weather; light to heavy and hard Most types easy to shape; hold on fasteners good; glue, paint and clear finish bond well	Furniture and cabinets; interior trim; flooring and staircases
Redwood	Yellow- to red-brown; even, straight grain Strong and rigid with high resistance to decay; low shrinkage and warpage when dried; light and fairly hard Easy to shape; hold on fasteners good; glue, paint and clear finish bond well	Exterior siding (shingles, shakes, clapboards); fences; decks
Spruce	Creamy white, often with hints of pink; even, straight grain Strong with low shrinkage and warpage when dried; light and soft Easy to shape; hold on fasteners good; paint bonds poorly	Rough framing (studs)
HARDWOOD		
Ash	White to dark brown; coarse, uneven, straight or wavy grain Strong with excellent bending qualities; heavy and hard Easy to shape; hold on fasteners good; glue, paint and clear finish bond well	Furniture (tabletops, chairs, bent parts, turnings) and cabinets
Birch	White to pale brown; fine, uneven, straight or wavy grain Strong with good bending qualities; heavy and hard Easy to shape; hold on fasteners good, but often splits when nailed or screwed; glue and paint bond poorly; clear finish bonds well	Furniture (chairs, bent parts, turnings) and cabinets; interior trim and paneling; interior doors; often used to imitate other types of wood
Cherry	Pale to dark red-brown, often with hints of green; fine, uneven, straight or wavy grain Strong with good bending qualities; moderately heavy and hard Easy to shape; hold on fasteners good: screws better than nails; glue and clear finish bond well	Quality furniture (tabletops, bent parts, turnings) and cabinets; often veneer
Mahogany	Brown to dark red-brown; fine, even, straight grain, often with vivid, flecked patterns Strong with good bending qualities; heavy and moderately hard Easy to shape, but tends to scuff when planed; hold on fasteners good: screws better than nails; glue and clear finish bond well	Quality furniture (tabletops, bent parts, turnings) and cabinets; interior trim and paneling; often veneer
Maple	White to pale red-brown; fine, even, straight grain, often with bird's eye or burl patterns Exceptionally strong with good bending qualities; heavy and hard Easy to shape; hold on fasteners good: screws better than nails; glue and clear finish bond well	Quality furniture (tabletops, bent parts, turnings) and cabinets; interior trim and paneling; flooring and staircases; often veneer
Oak	Pale gray to red-brown; coarse, even, straight grain, often with flecked patterns Strong with good bending qualities; heavy and very hard Hard to shape; hold on fasteners good, but often splits when nailed; glue and clear finish bond well	Quality furniture (tabletops) and cabinets; flooring and staircases; interior trim and paneling; interior doors; often veneer

TYPE	CHARACTERISTICS	USES
Rosewood	Dark brown to black, often with hints of dark purple or streaks of orange; coarse, uneven grain with highly-figured patterns Exceptionally strong with good bending qualities; heavy, hard and very oily Hard to shape, tending to dull blades; hold on fasteners good: screws better than nails; glue bonds well; usually finished with penetrating oil	Quality furniture and cabinets; flooring and staircases (borders of parquetry slats); often veneer
Teak	Medium to dark brown, often with hints of yellow; coarse, even, straight grain Strong with good bending qualities; heavy, very hard and oily Easy to shape, but tends to dull blades and suffer burn marks from power tools; hold on fasteners good; glue bonds well; usually finished with penetrating oil	Furniture and cabinets; often veneer
Walnut	Gray- to dark brown, often with hints of purple; coarse, even, straight grain Exceptionally strong with good bending qualities; moderately heavy and hard Easy to shape; hold on fasteners good; glue and clear finish bond well	Quality furniture (tabletops, bent parts, turnings) and cabinets; often veneer
BOARD PRODUCT		
Fiberboard	Weak, but fairly flexible; light and soft Easy to cut, but tends to shred; hold on fasteners poor; glue and paint bond well	Sheathing for exterior walls; insulation
Hardboard	Brittle; fairly heavy and hard Easy to cut, but tends to shred; hold on fasteners poor; glue and paint bond well	Exterior siding; flooring underlayment; interior paneling
Particleboard (chip; flake; oriented strand)	Fairly strong; fairly heavy and hard Easy to cut; hold on fasteners good; glue and paint bond well	Sheathing for exterior walls; subflooring; flooring underlayment
Plywood	Strong; heavy and fairly hard Easy to cut; hold on fasteners good; glue and paint bond well	Sheathing for exterior walls; subflooring; flooring underlayment; interior paneling

LUMBER SIZES: NOMINAL VERSUS ACTUAL

SOFTWOOD

NOMINAL (INCHES)	ACTUAL (INCHES)	
	DRY	GREEN
1-by-2	3/4-by-1 1/2	25/32-by-1 9/16
1-by-3	3/4-by-2 1/2	25/32-by-2 9/16
1-by-4	3/4-by-3 1/2	25/32-by-3 9/16
1-by-5	3/4-by-4 1/2	25/32-by-4 9/16
1-by-6	3/4-by-5 1/2	25/32-by-5 5/8
1-by-8	3/4-by-7 1/4	25/32-by-7 1/2
1-by-10	3/4-by-9 1/4	25/32-by-9 1/2
1-by-12	3/4-by-11 1/4	25/32-by-11 1/2
2-by-2	1 1/2-by-1 1/2	1 9/16-by-1 9/16
2-by-3	1 1/2-by-2 1/2	1 9/16-by-2 9/16
2-by-4	1 1/2-by-3 1/2	1 9/16-by-3 9/16
2-by-6	1 1/2-by-5 1/2	1 9/16-by-5 5/8
2-by-8	1 1/2-by-7 1/4	1 9/16-by-7 1/2
2-by-10	1 1/2-by-9 1/4	1 9/16-by-9 1/2
2-by-12	1 1/2-by-11 1/4	1 9/16-by-11 1/2
3-by-4	2 1/2-by-3 1/2	2 9/16-by-3 9/16
4-by-4	3 1/2-by-3 1/2	3 9/16-by-3 9/16

NOMINAL (INCHES)	ACTUAL (INCHES)	
	DRY	GREEN
4-by-6	3 1/2-by-5 1/2	3 9/16-by-5 5/8
6-by-6	5 1/2-by-5 1/2	5 5/8-by-5 5/8
8-by-8	7 1/4-by-7 1/4	7 1/2-by-7 1/2

HARDWOOD

NOMINAL (INCHES)	ACTUAL (INCHES)	
	SURFACED ONE SIDE	SURFACED TWO SIDES
3/8	1/4	3/16
1/2	3/8	5/16
5/8	1/2	7/16
3/4	5/8	9/16
1	7/8	13/16
1 1/4	1 1/8	1 1/16
1 1/2	1 3/8	1 5/16
2	1 13/16	1 3/4
3	2 13/16	2 3/4
4	3 13/16	3 3/4

LUMBER GRADES: SOFTWOOD AND PLYWOOD

TYPE	CHARACTERISTICS	USES
BOARDS: SELECT AND COMMON		
Select B and better (No. 1 and No. 2 clear)	Highest quality: very minor defects and blemishes Not always available; expensive	Trim; cabinetry; paneling; flooring; siding; decks
Select C (choice)	High quality: small defects and blemishes	Trim; cabinetry; paneling; flooring; siding; decks
Select D (quality)	Quality: defects and blemishes that can be concealed with paint or other finish	Trim; cabinetry; paneling; siding; decks
No. 1 common (colonial)	Small, minor defects and blemishes: tight knots up to 2 1/2 inches wide	Trim; paneling
No. 2 common (sterling)	Larger, coarser defects and blemishes than No. 1 common: tight knots up to 4 inches wide	Siding; paneling
No. 3 common (standard)	Larger, coarser defects and blemishes than No. 2 common: small knotholes	Sheathing (roofing, siding); fencing
No. 4 common (utility)	Larger, coarser defects and blemishes than No. 3 common: large knotholes	Sheathing (roofing, siding); fencing; subflooring
DIMENSION LUMBER		
No. 1 (construction)	Small, minor defects and blemishes: no knots wider than 1 1/2 inches No checks, splits or warping	Rough framing: headers; studs; top or sole plates; firestops; bridging; furring strips
No. 2 (standard)	Larger, coarser defects and blemishes than No. 1 common: knots wider than 2 inches or on edges; checks at ends No splits or warping	Rough framing: headers; studs; top or sole plates; firestops; bridging; furring strips
No. 3 (utility studs)	Larger, coarser defects and blemishes than No. 2 common: knotholes up to 1 1/2 inches wide; checks; splits; warping	Rough framing: studs; furring strips
Joists and planks	Free of defects that affect strength or rigidity	Load-bearing framing: joists; built-up girders
PLYWOOD: INTERIOR/EXPOSURE 1		
A-D	Grade A face; Grade D back and inner plies Few defects and blemishes on face: smooth; paintable Large, coarse defects and blemishes on back: knots or knotholes up to 2 1/2 inches wide; limited splits	General applications where appearance of only face important; paneling
CDX (rated sheathing)	Grade C face; Grade D back and inner plies Defects and blemishes on face: tight knots up to 1 1/2 inches wide; knotholes up to 1 inch wide; limited splits Large, coarse defects and blemishes on back: knots or knotholes up to 2 1/2 inches wide; limited splits	Sheathing; subflooring
Underlayment	Grade C plugged (knotholes filled) face; Grade D back; Grades C and D inner plies Surface defects and blemishes on face: knotholes (filled) up to 1/4-by-1/2 inch; splits up to 1/8 inch wide Large, coarse surface defects and blemishes on back: knots or knotholes up to 2 1/2 inches wide; limited splits	Underlayment (over subflooring) for resilient flooring, carpeting
PLYWOOD: EXTERIOR/EXPOSURE 2		
A-B	Grade A face; Grade B back; Grade C inner plies Few defects and blemishes on face: smooth; paintable Minor defects and blemishes on back: tight knots up to 1 inch wide; minor splits	General applications where appearance of only face important
A-C	Grade A face; Grade C back and inner plies Few defects and blemishes on face: smooth; paintable Defects and blemishes on back: tight knots up to 1 1/2 inches wide; knotholes up to 1 inch wide; limited splits	Soffits; fences
T 1-11 (rated siding)	Grade C face, back and inner plies; surface textured Defects and blemishes on face and back: tight knots up to 1 1/2 inches wide; knotholes up to 1 inch wide; limited splits	Siding; soffits; fences
Sturd-i-floor	Grade C plugged (knotholes filled) face; Grade D back; Grades C and D inner plies Defects and blemishes on face: knotholes (filled) up to 1/4-by-1/2 inch; splits up to 1/8 inch wide Large, coarse defects and blemishes on back: knots or knotholes up to 2 1/2 inches wide; limited splits	Decking; subflooring and underlayment for carpeting

BOARD DEFECTS

TYPE	CHARACTERISTICS	USES
Knot	Appears as dark whorl; varies in size from less than 1/2 inch wide (pin knot) to 1 1/2 inches wide	Up to 3/4 inch wide suitable for applications not load-bearing (studs, firestops, blocking) and where appearance not important
	Up to 3/4 inch wide does not weaken wood, but may mar its appearance; more than 3/4 inch substantially weakens wood, especially if at edge	
Reaction wood	Appears as compressed growth rings and dark streak in grain pattern; often found near knot	General applications where reaction wood will not be cut or shaped
	Weakens wood, making it brittle and shrink unevenly; difficult to cut	
Shake	Appears as wide crack, usually between growth rings	General applications where appearance not important
	Does not weaken wood, but may mar its appearance	
Check	Appears as small cracks across growth rings	General applications where appearance not important
	Does not weaken wood, but may mar its appearance	
Crook	Appears as end-to-end curve along edge	Suitable for applications load-bearing horizontally (joists) with convex side upward; weight eventually straightens board
	Weakens wood in applications load-bearing vertically; board difficult to cut	
Bow	Appears as end-to-end curve along face	Suitable for applications load-bearing horizontally (joists) with convex side upward; weight eventually straightens board
	Weakens wood in applications load-bearing vertically; board difficult to cut	
Twist	Appears as uneven or irregular warping	Suitable for applications not load-bearing (studs, firestops, blocking) and where straightness or appearance not important
	Weakens wood, making it unstable and prone to further warping as it dries	
Warp-prone end	Appears as growth rings at end parallel to face	Suitable for applications not load-bearing (studs, firestops, blocking) and where straightness or appearance not important
	Does not weaken wood, but tends to result in warping with humidity and temperature changes	
Pitch	Appears as accumulation of resin or "pitch pocket"	Suitable for applications where finish not needed
	Does not weaken wood, but makes surface tacky and messy; bleeds through finish	
Cross grain	Appears as grain not parallel to edge	Suitable for applications not load-bearing (studs, firestops, blocking)
	Weakens wood	

SHEET METAL

TYPE	CHARACTERISTICS	USES
Aluminum	Pure metal or stronger alloy; measured by decimal thickness Commonly available in sheets 2-by-6 feet; also in sheets 36-by-36 inches, 24-by-36 inches, 12-by-18 inches or 12-by-12 inches	Flashing; gutters and downspouts; roofing; siding
Copper	Pure metal; measured by Brown & Sharpe (B&S) or American Wire Gauge (AWG) number or weight Commonly available in rolls 2-by-8 feet; also in sheets 12-by-18 inches or 12-by-12 inches	Flashing; roofing
Galvanized steel	Steel plated with zinc; measured by U.S. Standard Gauge number Commonly available in rolls 2-by-8 feet	Flashing; gutters and downspouts; roofing
Tin	Steel plated with tin; measured by U.S. Standard Gauge number Commonly available in sheets 20-by-28 inches	Flashing; roofing

DRYWALL

TYPE	CHARACTERISTICS	USES
Standard panel	Width of 4 feet and length of 8 feet most common; lengths of 6, 7, 10, 12 or 16 feet also available Thickness of 1/4, 3/8, 1/2 or 5/8 inch Tapered edges most common; beveled, rounded, square, straight or tongue-and-groove edges also available	Interior applications in areas not subjected to moisture or fire hazard
Water-resistant panel	Width of 4 feet and length of 8 feet most common; lengths of 6, 7, 10, 12 or 16 feet also available Thickness of 1/4, 3/8, 1/2 or 5/8 inch Tapered edges most common; beveled, rounded, square, straight or tongue-and-groove edges also available	Interior applications in areas subjected to moisture (walls around bathtub or shower stall)
Type X fire-rated (firestop) panel	Width of 4 feet and length of 8 feet most common; lengths of 6, 7, 10, 12 or 16 feet also available Thickness of 1/4, 3/8, 1/2 or 5/8 inch Tapered edges most common; beveled, rounded, square, straight or tongue-and-groove edges also available	Interior applications in areas subjected to fire hazard (boiler room, garage or workshop)

BRICKS AND BLOCKS

TYPE	CHARACTERISTICS	USES
Standard building brick	Of clay or concrete; standard durability May be solid or cored; cored type for greatest resistance to lateral force (mortar trickles into holes)	Backing course of walls and chimney caps; paving of driveways, walkways and patios
Standard face brick	Of clay or concrete and available in variety of colors: red, brown, gray, white or gold; more durable and attractive than standard building type May be solid or cored; cored type for greatest resistance to lateral force (mortar trickles into holes)	Exposed course of walls and chimney caps; retaining walls
Pressed brick	Face brick with sharp edges, perfectly squared corners and smooth outer surface	Exposed course of walls and chimney caps
Glazed brick	Face brick with glazed surface; often white, but may be of other color	Exposed course of walls; applications where ease of cleaning important
Firebrick	Of fireclay to withstand high temperatures	Fireplace interior
Paving brick (paver)	Commonly of concrete; available in variety of sizes, shapes and colors	Paving of driveways, walkways and patios
Stretcher block	Commonly of concrete, but may be of clay, shale or slag; available in variety of sizes, shapes and surface textures May be solid or hollow (two or three cores separated by partitions called webs); may have mortar-joint projections at each end	Foundation walls; applications where appearance not important
Decorative block	Commonly of concrete and available in variety of sizes, shapes and surface textures Decorative core for appearance; permits penetration of light and circulation of air	Freestanding walls
Concrete edging	Precast borders of concrete available in variety of sizes and shapes	Perimeter of paving bricks; prevents spreading of paving bricks and erosion of sand bed

STONE

TYPE	CHARACTERISTICS	USE
Granite	Typically gray; often mixed with hues of brown, black, white, pink or red	Walls (including foundations): building Walkways, steps, patios
	Surface sparkles; non-porous	
	Heavy (170 pounds per cubic foot)	
	High strength and durability	
	Difficult to work and expensive; can be polished	
Limestone	Typically buff, cream, ivory, brown or green	Walls (excluding fire-resistant): building or veneer Walkways, steps, patios
	Surface chalky, often embedded with small fossils; porous (areas exposed to water virtually "self-cleaning") and sensitive to pollution (tending to crumble)	
	Heavy (170 pounds per cubic foot)	
	Low to moderate strength; moderate to high durability	
	Easy to work	
Marble	White when purest; often other colors with visible stripes	Flooring Countertops Walls: veneer Lintels (load-bearing pieces above doors and windows) Keystones (wedge-shaped, locking pieces at top of arches)
	Surface crystalline (similar to sugar); non-porous	
	Heavy (170 pounds per cubic foot)	
	Moderate to high strength and high durability	
	Difficult to work and expensive; usually polished	
Sandstone	Typically buff, cream, brown, gray-pink, red, or blue; hues of red depend on iron content	Walls (excluding foundations): building or veneer Sills (dry, no-frost areas)
	Surface rough, sandy; porous (areas exposed to water require cleaning to prevent embedded crusts of dirt)	
	Moderately heavy (150 pounds per cubic foot)	
	Strength and durability depend on hardness (soft seams that can be picked out with nail indicate poor quality)	
	Easy to work; hardest and finest-grained can be polished	
Slate	Typically black, gray, green, blue or blue-gray	Roofing Flooring Walls: veneer Walkways, steps, patios
	Surface skid-resistant; non-porous, dense and brittle	
	Heavy (175 pounds per cubic foot)	
	High strength and moderate durability	
	Easy to work; set flat, not on edge	

STONE FORMS

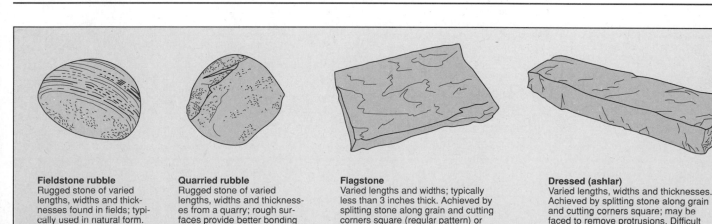

Fieldstone rubble
Rugged stone of varied lengths, widths and thicknesses found in fields; typically used in natural form.

Quarried rubble
Rugged stone of varied lengths, widths and thicknesses from a quarry; rough surfaces provide better bonding with mortar than weathered surfaces of fieldstone rubble.

Flagstone
Varied lengths and widths; typically less than 3 inches thick. Achieved by splitting stone along grain and cutting corners square (regular pattern) or irregular (mosaic design); usually faced to remove protrusions.

Dressed (ashlar)
Varied lengths, widths and thicknesses. Achieved by splitting stone along grain and cutting corners square; may be faced to remove protrusions. Difficult form to achieve; stone best prepared by professional.

MORTAR RECIPES

TYPE	INGREDIENTS	USES
M	Packaged mortar mix Water: until thick, buttery consistency that holds shape 1 part portland cement; 1/4 part hydrated lime; 3 parts sand Water: until thick, buttery consistency that holds shape 1 part portland cement; 1 part type II masonry cement; 6 parts sand Water: until thick, buttery consistency that holds shape	General interior masonry; exterior masonry below-ground or otherwise in contact with soil (foundations, retaining walls, walkways, patios): repointing or replacing bricks, blocks or stones; parging; building a cove on foundation footing
N	Packaged mortar mix Water: until thick, buttery consistency that holds shape 1 part portland cement; 1 part hydrated lime; 6 parts sand Water: until thick, buttery consistency that holds shape 1 part type II masonry cement; 3 parts sand Water: until thick, buttery consistency that holds shape	General interior masonry; exterior masonry above-ground subjected to extreme weathering: repointing or replacing bricks, blocks or stones
S	1 part portland cement; 1/2 part hydrated lime; 4 1/2 parts sand Water: until thick, buttery consistency that holds shape 1/2 part portland cement; 1 part type II masonry cement; 4 1/2 parts sand Water: until thick, buttery consistency that holds shape	Masonry subjected to extreme lateral force such as strong winds: repointing or replacing bricks, blocks or stones
Fireclay	Packaged fireclay mortar mix Water: until thick, buttery consistency that holds shape 1 part fireclay mortar; 3 parts sand Water: until thick, buttery consistency that holds shape	Interior masonry of fireplace subjected to extreme heat: repointing or replacing firebricks

CONCRETE AND STUCCO RECIPES

TYPE	INGREDIENTS	USES
Bonding slurry	Portland cement Water: until runny, creamy consistency	Surface-patching of interior or exterior masonry or concrete
Concrete	Packaged concrete mix Water: until thick consistency that flows without crumbling 1 part portland cement; 2 1/2 parts wet sand; aggregate: 1 1/2 parts 3/8-inch gravel, 2 parts 1/2-inch gravel or 2 1/2 parts 3/4-inch gravel Water: until thick consistency that flows without crumbling	Replacing section of exterior concrete (walkways, steps, patios, driveways)
Concrete patching mix	Latex concrete patching compound Water: until thick consistency that flows without crumbling; may be premixed 1 part portland cement; 2 1/2 parts fine sand Water: until thick consistency that flows without crumbling	General patching of interior or exterior concrete
Stucco	1 part portland cement; 1 part hydrated lime; 3 parts sand Water: until thick, buttery consistency that holds shape	Patching scratch or brown coat of high lime content
	1 part portland cement; 1/2 part hydrated lime; 3 parts sand Water: until thick, buttery consistency that holds shape	Patching scratch or brown coat of high portland cement content
	1 part portland cement; 1 1/2 parts hydrated lime; 3 parts fine sand Water: until thick, buttery consistency that holds shape	Patching finish coat of high lime content
	1 part portland cement; 1 part lime; 3 parts fine sand	Patching finish coat of high portland cement content

NAILS, TACKS AND POP RIVETS

TYPE	CHARACTERISTICS	USES
Common nail	Lengths from 1 inch to 12 inches; types 6 inches or longer called spikes Thick, grooved shank for strength and holding power; broad head prevents pulling through	General fastening of wood
Box nail	Lengths from 1 inch to 4 inches Thinner shank than common nail for less holding power; blunted tip less prone to splitting	General fastening of wood; hot-dipped, galvanized types for exterior
Finishing nail	Lengths from 1 1/2 to 4 inches; types less than 1 1/2 inches called brads Smooth shank; small, cupped head for concealing with nail set	General fastening of wood: light construction or carpentry; hardened types for hardwood
Casing nail	Lengths from 1 1/4 to 4 inches most common Slightly thicker shank than finishing nail for greater strength; small, cupped head for driving flush or concealing with nail set	General fastening of wood: light construction or carpentry
Brad (wire brad)	Lengths from 3/8 inch to 1 1/2 inches Small, thin type of finishing nail; small, cupped head for concealing with nail set	Interior fastening of wood: delicate carpentry
Spiral nail	Lengths from 1 1/4 to 12 inches (to 4 inches common) Spiral-threaded shank twists for screw-like grip and holding power; tapered head	General fastening of wood: heavy construction (framing); special types for siding (wood, vinyl, aluminum), hardwood flooring, masonry
Hardwood flooring nail	Lengths from 1 1/4 to 3 inches (2 1/4 and 2 1/2 inches common for tongue-and-groove flooring) Type of spiral nail: thin shank less prone to splitting; small, cupped head for concealing with nail set	Fastening of hardwood flooring
Siding nail	Lengths from 1 1/4 to 3 1/2 inches Type of spiral nail; flat head similar to box nail Annular ring types also available	Special types for fastening siding: wood, vinyl, aluminum
Annular ring (ring-shank) nail	Lengths from 1 1/4 to 8 inches Ringed shank for holding power	General fastening of board products: plywood, particleboard, hardboard or fiberboard; special types for drywall, paneling, flooring, siding, roofing
Drywall nail	Lengths from 1 1/4 to 2 inches Resin-coated type of annular ring nail; tapered head for dimpling surface	Fastening of drywall
Roofing nail	Lengths from 1/2 inch to 3 inches (straw nail to 5 inches) Galvanized for rust-resistance: smooth shank; broad, flat head Spiral and annular ring types also available; some types fitted with lead or plastic washer	Special types for fastening roofing: asphalt shingles, wood shakes or shingles, slates, flashing; straw type with 5-inch shank for clay tiles
Self-furring nail	Provides holding power at set distance (equal to plug length) from surface	Fastening of metal lath; plug positioned behind lath and nail driven into it
Duplex (scaffold) nail	Lengths from 1 3/4 to 4 inches Double-headed type of common nail; second head prevents pulling through and easy removal	General fastening of wood temporarily
Masonry nail	Lengths from 3/4 inch to 4 inches Fluted or spiral shank for holding power; flat head	Fastening to masonry or concrete; special concrete screw-nail type for fastening to cured concrete
Carpet tack	Lengths from 7/16 to 5/8 inch Short shank; broad, flat head	Fastening of staircase runners
Pop rivet	Sized from No. 1 to No. 4 for thickness of 1/4 to 5/8 inch; diameter of 1/8 or 1/4 inch Long, thin mandrel; short, thick head	Fastening of metal, vinyl and plastic with pop riveter

NAIL SIZES: COMMON, FINISHING AND CASING

COMMON NAILS

| "PENNY" RATING | LENGTH | DIAMETER | |
	INCHES	SHANK (GAUGE NUMBER)	HEAD (INCHES)
2d	1	15	11/64
3d	1 1/4	14	13/64
4d	1 1/2	12 1/2	7/32
5d	1 3/4	12 1/2	15/64
6d	2	11 1/2	1/4
7d	2 1/4	11 1/2	17/64
8d	2 1/2	10 1/4	9/32
9d	2 3/4	10 1/4	9/32
10d	3	9	5/16
12d	3 1/4	9	5/16
16d	3 1/2	8	11/32
20d	4	6	13/32
30d	4 1/2	5	7/16
40d	5	4	15/32
50d	5 1/2	3	1/2
60d	6	2	17/32

FINISHING NAILS

| "PENNY" RATING | LENGTH | DIAMETER (GAUGE NUMBER) | |
	INCHES	SHANK	HEAD
2d	1	16 1/2	13 1/2
3d	1 1/4	15 1/2	12 1/2
4d	1 1/2	15	12
5d	1 3/4	15	12
6d	2	13	10
8d	2 1/2	12 1/2	9 1/2
10d	3	11 1/2	8 1/2
16d	3 1/2	11	8
20d	4	10	7

CASING NAILS

| "PENNY" RATING | LENGTH | DIAMETER (GAUGE NUMBER) | |
	INCHES	SHANK	HEAD
4d	1 1/2	14	11
6d	2	12 1/2	9 1/2
8d	2 1/2	11 1/2	8 1/2
10d	3	10 1/2	7 1/2
16d	3 1/2	10	7

ACTUAL NAIL SIZES: COMMON, FINISHING AND CASING

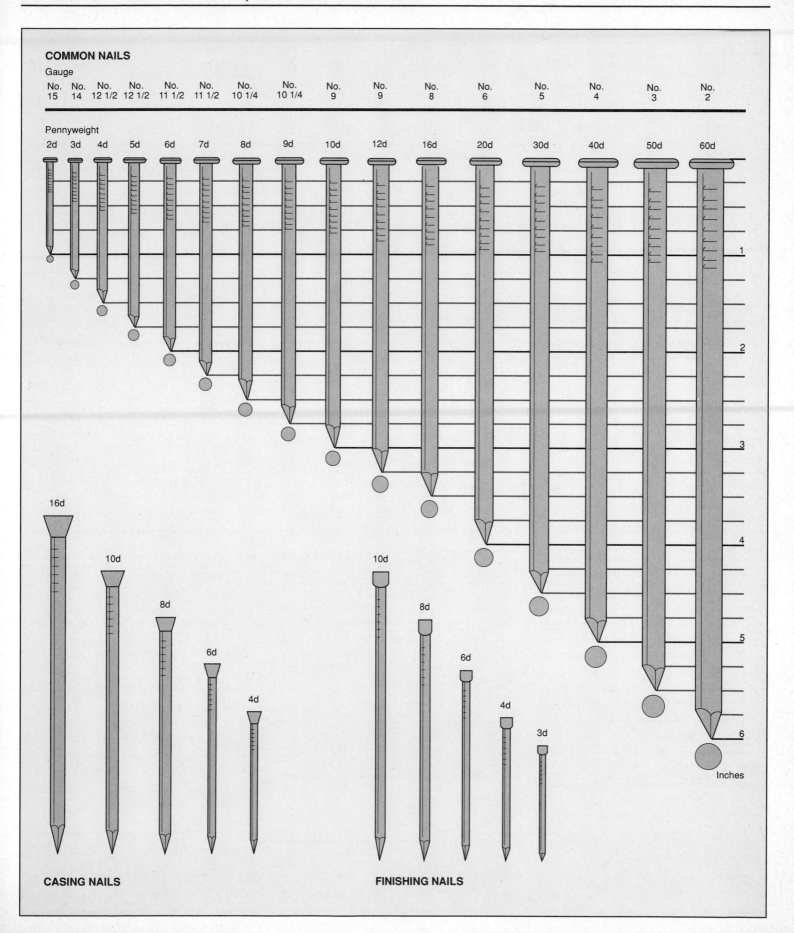

COMMON NAILS

Gauge

No. 15	No. 14	No. 12 1/2	No. 12 1/2	No. 11 1/2	No. 11 1/2	No. 10 1/4	No. 10 1/4	No. 9	No. 9	No. 8	No. 6	No. 5	No. 4	No. 3	No. 2

Pennyweight

| 2d | 3d | 4d | 5d | 6d | 7d | 8d | 9d | 10d | 12d | 16d | 20d | 30d | 40d | 50d | 60d |

1

2

3

4

5

6

Inches

CASING NAILS

16d

10d

8d

6d

4d

FINISHING NAILS

10d

8d

6d

4d

3d

SCREWS

TYPE	CHARACTERISTICS	USES
Wood screw	Usually available in lengths from 1/2 inch to 6 inches; diameters from No. 0 to No. 24 (gauges) (.06 to .372 inch) Most common head types: slotted; Phillips (cross recess); Robertson (square recess) Variety of head shapes: flat for countersinking and concealing; oval for countersinking and appearance; round for easy removal Threaded shank provides greater holding power than nail	Fastening through wood or other material to wood Fastening through light wood or other material to masonry (with anchor or shield)
Lag bolt (lag screw)	Usually available in lengths from 1 inch to 12 inches; diameters from 1/4 to 3/4 inch Most common head shapes: hex; square Thick, threaded shank provides greater strength and holding power than wood or masonry screw	Fastening through heavy wood or other material to wood (with washer under head) Fastening through heavy wood or other material to masonry (with anchor or shield)
Drywall screw	Usually available in diameter (gauge) ranges: No. 6 in lengths from 1 inch to 2 1/4 inches; No. 8 in lengths of 2 1/2 or 3 inches; No. 10 in lengths of 3 3/4 inches Head flat; bugle-shaped	Fastening through drywall to wood or metal
Type A sheet metal screw	Usually available in lengths from 1/4 inch to 3 inches; diameters from No. 2 to No. 14 (gauges) and of 5/16 and 3/8 inch Most common head shapes: flat; pan; round; hex	Fastening through sheet metal to metal or wood Fastening plywood or other board product to wood
Type F sheet metal screw	Usually available in lengths from 3/16 inch to 3 inches; diameters from No. 4 to No. 10 (gauges) and of 1/4, 5/16 and 3/8 inch Most common head shapes: flat; pan; round; hex	Fastening through material to metal or plastic .05 to 1/2 inch thick
Masonry screw	Usually available in lengths from 1 1/4 to 4 inches; diameters No. 12 and No. 14 (gauges) (3/16 and 1/4 inch) Most common head shapes: flat for countersinking and concealing; hex-washer for easy removal	Fastening through material to masonry
One-way high-security screw	Usually available in lengths from 1/2 inch to 3 inches; diameters from No. 4 to No. 14 (gauges) (1/8 to 1/4 inch) Head design permits screw to be tightened, not removed	Fastening lock hardware to wood

ACTUAL SCREW SIZES: SLOTTED-HEAD

HEAD	SHANK	GAUGE	HEAD	SHANK	GAUGE	HEAD	SHANK	GAUGE
		No. 0			No. 8			No. 16
		No. 1			No. 9			No. 18
		No. 2			No. 10			No. 20
		No. 3			No. 12			No. 24
		No. 4			No. 14			
		No. 5						
		No. 6						
		No. 7						

ANCHORS AND SHIELDS

TYPE	CHARACTERISTICS	USES
Plastic anchor	Sized to match diameter of screw Good hold for moderate load on drywall or plaster; light load on masonry or ceramic tile; very light load on ceiling	With screw for fastening material to drywall, plaster, ceramic tile or masonry
Plastic anchor (hammer-driven type)	Sized to match diameter of screw Good hold for light load on drywall or plaster; very light load on ceiling	With screw for fastening material to drywall or plaster
Fiber anchor or shield	Sized to match diameter of screw Good hold for light load on drywall or plaster; moderate load on masonry or ceramic tile; very light load on ceiling	With screw for fastening material to drywall, plaster, ceramic tile or masonry
Lead or alloy anchor or shield	Sized to match diameter of lag bolt or other screw Good hold for heavy load on masonry or concrete	With lag bolt or other screw for fastening material to masonry or concrete
Expansion anchor (sleeve type)	Comes with sleeve in four common sizes for different thicknesses: XS for up to 1/4 inch; S for 1/8 to 5/8 inch; L for 5/8 inch to 1 1/4 inches; XL for 1 1/4 to 1 3/4 inches Good hold for moderate load on drywall, plaster, ceramic tile or concrete block; light load on ceiling	Fastening material to drywall, plaster, ceramic tile or hollow concrete block; must penetrate to hollow cavity
Expansion anchor (sleeveless type)	Comes in four common sizes for different thicknesses: XS for up to 1/4 inch; S for 1/8 to 5/8 inch; L for 5/8 inch to 1 1/4 inches; XL for 1 1/4 to 1 3/4 inches Good hold for light load on drywall, plaster, ceramic tile or concrete block; very light load on ceiling	Fastening material to drywall, plaster, ceramic tile or hollow concrete block; must penetrate to hollow cavity
Expansion anchor (hammer-driven type)	Comes with sleeve in four common sizes for different thicknesses: XS for up to 1/4 inch; S for 1/8 to 5/8 inch; L for 5/8 inch to 1 1/4 inches; XL for 1 1/4 to 1 3/4 inches Good hold for light load on drywall or plaster; very light load on ceiling	Fastening material to drywall or plaster; must penetrate to hollow cavity

BOLTS

TYPE	CHARACTERISTICS	USES
Carriage bolt	Lengths from 1/2 inch to 18 inches (1 1/2 to 6 inches common); diameters from 1/4 to 3/4 inch (1/4 to 5/8 inch common) Round head with square or finned neck; coarse-threaded type most common	With nut for fastening wood or metal to wood: flat or platform washer and lock washer behind nut
Machine bolt	Lengths from 1/2 inch to 24 inches (1/2 inch to 8 inches common); diameters from 1/4 inch to 1 1/4 inches Hex or square head; coarse-threaded type most common (shank of large size not fully threaded)	With nut for fastening combinations of wood, metal or plastic: flat or platform washer behind head; flat or platform washer and lock washer behind nut
Stove bolt	Lengths from 3/4 inch to 6 inches (3/4 inch to 4 inches common); diameters from 1/8 to 1/2 inch (1/8 to 3/8 inch common) Slotted, flat or round head; coarse-threaded type most common	With nut for fastening combinations of light wood, metal or plastic: flat or platform washer behind head; flat or platform washer and lock washer behind nut
Toggle bolt	Lengths from 2 to 6 inches; diameters from 1/8 to 1/2 inch Slotted, round head; headless-shank type also available	Fastening light wood, metal or plastic to hollow wall or ceiling

NUTS

TYPE	CHARACTERISTICS	USES
Cap nut	Diameters from No. 6 (gauge) to 1/2 inch; typically coarse-threaded Cap covers sharp end of bolt, limiting tightening of nut; hex nut provides easy access for turning, but limited surface for gripping	Applications with bolt of minimum length where safety or appearance important
Hex nut	Variety of sizes to match diameter of bolts (bolts of hot-dipped galvanized steel typically supplied with required oversized type); coarse- and fine-threaded types common Hex shape provides easy access for turning, but limited surface for gripping	General applications with bolt
Square nut	Variety of sizes to match diameter of bolts; typically coarse-threaded Less common than hex nut; square shape provides limited access for turning, but maximum surface for gripping	General applications with bolt
Stop nut	Diameters from No. 4 to No. 10 (gauge) and 1/4 to 1 inch; coarse- and fine-threaded types common Held tight by nylon insert; loses holding power if removed and reinstalled more than two or three times	Applications with bolt where disassembly and reassembly not expected
T nut	Diameters from No. 6 (gauge) to 1/4 inch; typically coarse-threaded Points of base embed into wood	Blind applications with bolt—where its threads are not accessible after assembly
Wing nut	Diameters from No. 6 (gauge) to 3/4 inch; typically coarse-threaded Winged shape permits turning by hand	Applications with bolt where disassembly and reassembly expected

WASHERS

TYPE	CHARACTERISTICS	USES
Flat washer	Variety of sizes to match diameter of bolts; smaller surface area and less load distribution than platform washer	Placed behind head of bolt and/or behind nut to help distribute load
Platform washer	Variety of sizes to match diameter of bolts; larger surface area and greater load distribution than flat washer	Placed behind head of bolt and/or behind nut to help distribute load
Lock washer (friction type)	Variety of sizes with internal or external teeth to match diameter of bolts; provides less holding power than split-type lock washer	Placed behind nut to help keep it from loosening
Lock washer (split type)	Variety of sizes to match diameter of bolts; provides greater holding power than friction-type lock washer	Placed behind nut to help keep it from loosening

FASTENING HARDWARE: ANCHORS, BRACES AND HANGERS

ANCHORS

Post anchor (flange-type)
Anchors bottom of post to concrete footing; flanges set in concrete and anchor bolted to post.

Post anchor (bolt-type)
Anchors bottom of post to concrete footing or header; bolt of base set in concrete or base bolted to header and anchor fastened to post with framing-anchor nails.

BRACES

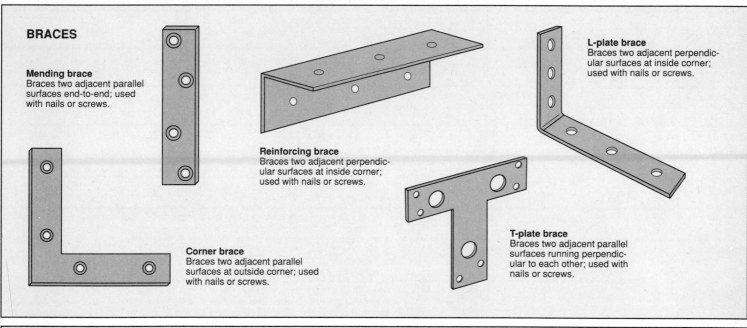

Mending brace
Braces two adjacent parallel surfaces end-to-end; used with nails or screws.

Reinforcing brace
Braces two adjacent perpendicular surfaces at inside corner; used with nails or screws.

Corner brace
Braces two adjacent parallel surfaces at outside corner; used with nails or screws.

L-plate brace
Braces two adjacent perpendicular surfaces at inside corner; used with nails or screws.

T-plate brace
Braces two adjacent parallel surfaces running perpendicular to each other; used with nails or screws.

HANGERS

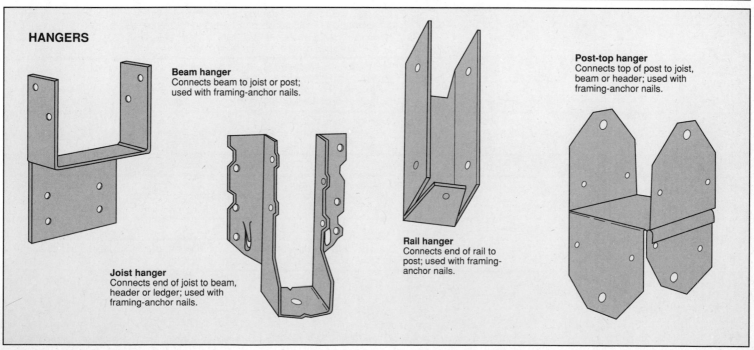

Beam hanger
Connects beam to joist or post; used with framing-anchor nails.

Joist hanger
Connects end of joist to beam, header or ledger; used with framing-anchor nails.

Rail hanger
Connects end of rail to post; used with framing-anchor nails.

Post-top hanger
Connects top of post to joist, beam or header; used with framing-anchor nails.

ABRASIVES

TYPE	GRIT	GRADE	USES
SANDPAPER			
Very coarse	20	3 1/2	Fast, heavy removing of material or many thick layers of finish
	30	2 1/2	With belt sander: rough sanding or trimming
	36	2	With drum sander and floor edger: first pass on wood flooring in poor condition
	40	1 1/2	
	50	1	
Coarse	60	1/2	Moderate to light removing of material or thick layers of finish
	80	1/0 (0)	Preliminary smoothing; leveling of deep depressions or scratches. With belt sander: intermediate smoothing. With drum sander and floor edger: second pass on wood flooring in poor condition; only pass on wood flooring in average condition
Medium	100	2/0	Light removing of material or thick layer of finish
	120	3/0	Intermediate smoothing; leveling of shallow depressions or scratches. With belt sander: final smoothing
Fine	150	4/0	Final smoothing before applying paint
	180	5/0	Light sanding or abrading between coats of paint
Very fine	220	6/0	Final smoothing before applying clear finish
	240	7/0	Light sanding or abrading between coats of clear finish
Extra fine	280	8/0	Fine sanding or abrading to remove air bubbles between coats of clear finish
	320	9/0	
Super fine	400	10/0	Fine sanding or abrading to remove flaws before applying last coat of lacquer. Deglossing paint or clear finish
STEEL WOOL			
Very coarse		3	Fast, heavy removing of material or many thick layers of finish. Rough shaping or trimming
Coarse		2	Moderate to light removing of material or thick layers of finish. Preliminary smoothing; leveling of deep depressions or scratches
Medium		1	Light removing of material or thick layer of finish. Intermediate smoothing; leveling of shallow depressions or scratches. Preliminary wiping of residue off wood stripped with chemical stripper
Medium fine or fine		1/0 (0)	Final smoothing before applying paint. Light abrading between coats of paint. Heavy cleaning: deep stains or scuff marks
Very fine		2/0 (00)	General smoothing or abrading. Final cleaning of residue off wood stripped with chemical stripper. Deglossing paint or clear finish. Light cleaning: surface stains or scuff marks
Extra fine		3/0 (000)	Final smoothing before applying clear finish. Light abrading between coats of clear finish. Deglossing paint or clear finish; with lubricant to spot-repair clear finish. Cleaning of paint spots; general polishing of metal
Super fine		4/0 (0000)	Applying stain, wax or oil. Fine abrading of paint or clear finish to reduce gloss or sheen. Fine polishing of metal
SANDING SCREEN			
Medium	100		With commercial floor polisher: final pass on wood flooring to remove marks of drum sander and floor edger before applying clear finish; only pass on wood flooring in good condition before refinishing with clear finish of same type
	120		
SCRUBBING PAD			
			With commercial floor polisher: light sanding or abrading of wood flooring between coats of clear finish

WOOD PATCHING COMPOUNDS

TYPE	CHARACTERISTICS	USES
Wax stick (putty stick)	Wax-based; available in variety of wood colors Accepts stain and finish other than lacquer (can be applied after clear finish); very easy to apply	Filling nail and screw heads; shallow scratches; narrow cracks; small nicks and holes
Shellac stick	Shellac-based; available in variety of colors and sheens Accepts stain and finish; difficult to apply, especially vertically	Spot-repairing or perfecting clear finish
Wood putty	Water-based; pre-colored or color added before use Dries hard; cleans up easily with water Accepts stain and finish; easy to apply	Filling deep scratches; wide cracks; large or deep dents, gouges and holes
Wood dough (plastic wood filler)	Solvent-based; may be pre-colored Sets quickly and dries very hard; cleans up with mineral spirits Accepts paint; difficult to apply evenly and sand	Filling wide cracks; large or deep dents, gouges and holes
Sawdust and wood glue	Mixture of sawdust from wood being repaired and wood glue Accepts stain and finish; easy to apply	Filling narrow cracks and gaps; tiny holes
Epoxy preservative	Mixture of resin and hardener with preservative additives Strengthens wood fibers damaged by rot; easy to apply	Reinforcing spongy or pitted wood fibers prior to patching with filler
Epoxy patching compound	Mixture of resin and hardener Holds shape and dries exceptionally hard; water resistant Accepts paint; easy to apply	Filling wide cracks and gaps; large or deep dents, gouges and holes Rebuilding missing section

DRYWALL AND PLASTER PATCHING COMPOUNDS

TYPE	CHARACTERISTICS	USES
Joint compound	Base of gypsum or vinyl latex with retardant to slow setting Available ready-mixed Excellent in very thin coats; tends to shrink as it dries Very spreadable and sandable Setting time varies—typically 12 to 24 hours	Patching hairline cracks; superficial scratches; tiny nicks and holes Repeated thin coats for patching narrow cracks; shallow scratches; small or superficial dents, gouges and holes Applying finish coat; taping joints; installing corner bead
Spackling compound	Base of vinyl latex with calcium carbonate or of acrylic latex Available ready-mixed Good in thin coats; tends to shrink slightly as it dries Very spreadable and sandable Setting time varies—typically 8 to 24 hours	Patching narrow cracks; shallow scratches; small dents, gouges and holes Repeated coats for patching wide cracks; deep scratches; large or deep dents, gouges and holes Applying finish coat; installing corner bead
Vinyl spackling compound	Base of vinyl latex with gypsum and silicone Available ready-mixed Not good in thin coats; slight shrinkage as it dries Spreadable and sandable Setting time typically 24 hours	Patching narrow or wide cracks; shallow or deep scratches; small and shallow or large and deep dents, gouges and holes
General-purpose patching compound	Base of gypsum with vinyl additives Stronger than joint compound or spackling compound Difficult to apply in thin coats; minimal shrinkage as it dries Spreadable and sandable Setting time typically 3 hours	Patching wide cracks; deep scratches; large or deep dents, gouges and holes Not suitable for applying finish coat
Rapid-setting patching compound	Base of gypsum with vinyl additives, lime and calcium sulfate Available ready-mixed Stronger than joint compound or spackling compound Difficult to apply in thin coats; minimal shrinkage as it dries Spreadable and sets hard; difficult to sand Setting time varies—typically 25 to 90 minutes	Patching wide cracks; deep scratches; large or deep dents, gouges and holes Installing corner bead Not suitable for applying finish coat
Plaster of paris	Almost pure gypsum; may contain retardant to slow setting Good in thin coats; minimal shrinkage as it dries Spreadable and sandable; dries smooth and snow white Setting time typically 2 to 15 minutes; cold water or vinegar can be used to retard setting	Patching ornamental plaster moldings: cornices; medallions
Perlite plaster	Base of mortar with large proportion of perlite (expanded volcanic glass) for light weight Cannot be applied in thin coats; minimal shrinkage as it dries Spreadable and sets hard, rough and gritty; difficult to sand Setting time typically 24 hours	Preliminary filling of large or deep dents, gouges and holes in drywall, plaster, masonry or wood prior to filling with other patching compound

CONCRETE PATCHING COMPOUNDS

TYPE	CHARACTERISTICS	USES
Standard patching compound	Cement powder and sand with additives and bonding agent; water added prior to use	Interior and exterior patching of small holes and narrow cracks in concrete: walls; floors; driveways; walkways; patios
Latex patching compound	Cement powder and latex; mixed together prior to use Better adhesion than standard patching compound; can be applied thinly Sets very quickly	Interior and exterior patching of hairline cracks and rough spots in concrete: walls; floors; driveways; walkways; patios
Vinyl patching compound	Cement powder with additives and bonding agent; water added prior to use Better adhesion and bonding than standard patching compound; can be applied thinly	Interior and exterior patching of narrow cracks in concrete; also hairline cracks in masonry, ceramic tile, glass and marble
Epoxy patching compound	Cement powder, resin and hardener; mixed together prior to use Strong, water-resistant bonding	General interior and exterior patching of concrete where strength important; also bonding of broken pieces of concrete, masonry, steel and glass
Hydraulic cement	Cement powder with additives and bonding agent; ready-mixed or water added prior to use Strong, waterproof bonding; sets very quickly and expands slightly after application	Interior patching of wet, leaking cracks in concrete and masonry
Anchoring cement	Cement powder with additives and bonding agent; ready-mixed or water added prior to use Strong bonding; sets quickly and expands after application	Interior and exterior anchoring of metal or other material in concrete or masonry: bolts; posts

GLUES AND ADHESIVES

TYPE	CHARACTERISTICS	USES
White glue	Polyvinyl-acetate based; not toxic or flammable Average bonding; allows for working time of 15 to 20 minutes Setting time of about 2 hours; cures fully in 24 hours Dries clear, but does not sand well	General interior applications with wood
Yellow glue	Aliphatic-resin based; not toxic or flammable Stronger bonding than white glue; allows for working time of 3 to 5 minutes Setting time of about 30 minutes; cures fully in 24 hours Does not dry clear, but sands well	General interior applications with wood
Contact cement	Solvent based; toxic and may be flammable Strong bonding almost instantly; allows for no working time once materials contact Setting time of 10 to 30 minutes; cures fully in 24 hours	Interior applications with wood and plastic where little bond stress expected: veneers; laminates
Exterior wood glue	Polymer based; not toxic or flammable Strong, waterproof bonding; allows for working time of 5 to 25 minutes Setting time of 2 to 3 hours; cures fully in 24 hours	General exterior applications with wood
Epoxy glue	Resin and hardener typically mixed together prior to use; not flammable, but may be toxic Strong, waterproof bonding; allows for working time of 5 minutes to 2 hours (depending on type) Setting time of 5 minutes to 2 hours (depending on type); typically cures fully in 24 hours	Interior and exterior applications with most materials where strong, waterproof bond important: wood; metal; plastic; fiberglass; glass
Instant glue	Cyanoacrylate based; not toxic or flammable Strong, waterproof bonding; allows for working time of 10 to 60 seconds (depending on type) Setting time of 10 to 60 seconds (depending on type); typically cures fully in 24 hours	Interior and exterior applications with most non-porous materials where strong, waterproof bond important
Roofing cement (plastic cement)	Asphalt, tar, fiber or neoprene-rubber based; toxic and flammable Strong, waterproof bonding; allows for working time of several hours until it starts to set (remains pliable and flexible)	Exterior applications with roofing materials: asphalt type for other than built-up roofing; tar type for only built-up roofing; fiber type for only metal roofing; neoprene-rubber type for all roofing

CAULKS

TYPE	CHARACTERISTICS	USES
Butyl rubber	Available in white or gray; paintable with latex or alkyd paint Durable; excellent adhesion and fair shrinkage resistance Flexible (expands and contracts); stickiness and stringiness make application messy	Exterior applications that undergo expansion and contraction where appearance not important: typically joints of wood or metal and metal or masonry
Silicone rubber	Available in clear and colors: white, black, gray, bronze and brown common; paintable with alkyd paint Very durable (clear moderately durable); good adhesion (excellent with primer) and excellent shrinkage resistance Flexible (expands and contracts); strong odor until dry	Interior and exterior applications that undergo expansion and contraction where appearance important: typically joints of wood, metal, glass, porcelain or fiberglass and wood, metal, masonry or ceramic tile; small holes in metal
Styrene copolymer	Synthetic rubber or polyurethane based available in variety of colors; paintable with latex paint Very durable; excellent adhesion, but poor shrinkage resistance Flexible (expands and contracts); dries slowly	Exterior applications to vinyl or aluminum: joints; small holes Polyurethane type as seal against radon gas
Acrylic latex	Available in variety of colors; paintable with latex or alkyd paint Durable; excellent adhesion (good adhesion to metal with primer) and fair shrinkage resistance Moderately flexible (expands and contracts slightly); dries quickly and odorlessly	Interior and exterior applications that undergo limited expansion and contraction: typically joints of wood, metal or glass and wood, metal or masonry
Vinyl latex	Available in variety of colors; paintable with latex or alkyd paint Fairly durable; good adhesion (except to metal) and moderate shrinkage resistance Not flexible (dries hard and may become brittle); dries quickly and almost odorlessly	Interior applications that undergo little expansion and contraction: typically narrow joints of wood or metal and wood or glass
Vinyl acrylic	Available in variety of colors; paintable with latex or alkyd paint Durable; good adhesion and fair shrinkage resistance Moderately flexible (expands and contracts slightly); dries quickly and odorlessly	Interior and exterior applications that undergo limited expansion and contraction: typically joints of wood or metal and wood or metal
Concrete latex	Available in gray (dries to match concrete); paintable with latex or alkyd paint Very durable; excellent adhesion and shrinkage resistance Flexible (expands and contracts); dries quickly and odorlessly	Interior and exterior applications to concrete: hairline cracks

SEALANTS

TYPE	CHARACTERISTICS	USES
Asphalt paint	Black, asphalt-based coating: enamel or non-fibered; waterproof	Exterior metal where appearance not important: joints; cracks; pinholes
Asphalt crack sealant	Black, tar-based coating; dries to matte, textured finish of asphalt	Exterior asphalt: cracks; small holes
Polyurethane spray foam	Polyurethane-based foam that expands on application; insulates	Interior gaps: wood trim; framing
Acrylic resin	Mixture of portland cement and rubber; protects against stains, moisture penetration and weathering	Interior and exterior masonry
Epoxy resin	Epoxy-based coating that sets quickly; protects against stains, moisture penetration and weathering	Interior and exterior masonry
Silicone sealant	Silicone paint-like coating; protects against stains, moisture penetration and weathering	Interior and exterior masonry
Cement latex	Cement-based coating with latex additives; protects against stains, moisture penetration and weathering	Interior and exterior masonry
Cement mortar	Cement powder mixed with water in equal proportions; protects against stains, moisture penetration and weathering	Interior and exterior masonry
Bituminous sealant	Black, tar-based coating applied hot or cold; protects against stains, moisture penetration and weathering	Exterior masonry

FINISH STRIPPERS

TYPE	CHARACTERISTICS	USES
Ammoniated cleanser	Leaves paint; wood stain Not flammable; may be toxic Can be diluted with hot water for cleaning or spot-refinishing	Removing shellac, lacquer or varnish; buffing wax
Trisodium phosphate	Leaves paint; wood stain Not flammable; may be toxic Can be diluted with hot water for cleaning or spot-refinishing	Removing shellac, lacquer or varnish; buffing wax
Mineral spirits	Leaves paint; clear finish; wood stain Not flammable, but can burn; may be toxic	Removing buffing wax
Denatured alcohol	Leaves paint; wood stain Not flammable; may be toxic Can be diluted with lacquer thinner for cleaning or spot-refinishing	Removing shellac; buffing wax
Lacquer thinner	Leaves paint; wood stain Flammable and toxic; applied only in well-ventilated area	Removing shellac or lacquer; buffing wax
Methylene chloride	Strips wood bare Not flammable, but highly toxic; applied only in well-ventilated area	Removing paint; shellac, lacquer, varnish or polyurethane; buffing wax; wood stain
Methanol-toluol-acetone	Strips wood bare Flammable and highly toxic; applied only in well-ventilated area	Removing paint; shellac, lacquer, varnish or polyurethane; buffing wax; wood stain

INTERIOR WOOD STAINS

TYPE	CHARACTERISTICS	USES
PENETRATING		
Alcohol-based stain	Does not raise grain; fades in direct sunlight Does not bleed through clear finish of lacquer, varnish or polyurethane; does not accept shellac Difficult to apply evenly; dries in 15 minutes	Green-hued woods: ash; oak Fine, close-grained woods: birch; maple
Oil-based stain	Does not raise grain; does not fade in direct sunlight Does not bleed through clear finish Easy to apply evenly: saturates quickly and can over-emphasize grain pattern, producing zebra effect; dries in 24 hours	Light-colored hardwoods: ash; birch Coarse, open-grained hardwoods: butternut; oak; walnut Not recommended for softwoods: fir; pine
NGR (non-grain-raising) solvent-based stain	Does not raise grain; does not fade in direct sunlight Does not bleed through clear finish Difficult to apply evenly; dries in 1 hour	Attractive, wavy-or pattern-grained hardwoods: cherry; mahogany; maple Not recommended for softwoods: fir; pine
Water-based stain	Raises grain (surfaces require smoothing after application); does not fade in direct sunlight Does not bleed through clear finish Easy to apply evenly; dries in 24 hours	Even, straight-grained woods: cherry; mahogany; walnut
NON-PENETRATING		
Oil-based stain	Obscures grain, making different woods look alike Does not raise grain; does not fade in direct sunlight Does not bleed through clear finish Easy to apply evenly; dries in 12 to 24 hours	Close-grained woods: birch; cherry; pine Not recommended for open-grained hardwoods: oak; walnut

EXTERIOR WOOD STAINS AND PRESERVATIVES

TYPE	CHARACTERISTICS	USES
Opaque stain	Latex or alkyd base Pigments color wood and obscure grain Non-penetrating; dyes coat wood surface	Exterior wood: porches; decks; fences; roofing (fascias, eaves); siding
Semi-transparent penetrating stain	Alkyd base; may contain water repellents, fungicides and mildewcides Pigments color wood without completely obscuring grain Penetrates; dyes absorbed into wood fibers	Exterior wood: porches; decks; fences; roofing (fascias, eaves); siding
Preservative	Water repellents often with organic arsenic, fungicides, mildewcides, waxes or solvents; may be pigmented or temporarily darken wood Eventually weathers to natural wood color	Exterior wood where protection against moisture important: porches; decks; fences; roofing (fascias, eaves); siding

WOOD SEALERS

WOOD STAIN	SEALER SOLUTION	SEALER APPLICATION
Alcohol-based stain; NGR (non-grain-raising) stain	1 part shellac and 8 parts denatured alcohol	Brush onto wood surface before applying stain
Oil-based stain	1 part boiled linseed oil and 1 part mineral spirits	Wipe onto wood surface before applying stain
Water-based stain	None applicable	None applicable
CLEAR FINISH		
Shellac; lacquer	1 part shellac and 8 parts denatured alcohol	Brush onto wood surface before applying finish
Varnish	1 part varnish and 1 part mineral spirits	Brush onto wood surface before applying finish
Polyurethane	1 part polyurethane and 1 part mineral spirits	Brush onto wood surface before applying finish

An undercoat for wood stain or clear finish. Sealers serve several useful functions in finishing or refinishing wood. Apply a sealer before a wood stain or a clear finish to prevent resins in softwoods from bleeding into it. Applied before a wood stain, a sealer reduces its penetration into the wood; applied after a wood stain, a sealer prevents it from bleeding into the finish. Applied before a finish, a sealer provides a base for it.

CLEAR FINISHES

TYPE	CHARACTERISTICS	USES
BUFFING WAX	Produces bright sheen, enhancing color and grain Fair resistance to moisture; protects penetrating finish Fair durability; requires regular cleaning, buffing and reapplication Available in liquid or paste; easy to apply and touch up	Interior wood as protection for penetrating finish
PENETRATING FINISH		
Boiled linseed oil	Produces soft, deep luster, enhancing color (amber hues) and grain Low resistance to moisture; requires buffing wax for protection Low durability; requires regular reapplication Incompatible with clear finish of shellac or polyurethane Available in liquid; easy to apply and touch up	Interior wood in areas not prone to wear or moisture
Rubbing or antiquing oil	Produces soft, deep luster, enhancing color and grain; can be rubbed to varying degrees of sheen Fair resistance to moisture; requires buffing wax for protection Good durability; requires periodic reapplication Incompatible with clear finish of shellac Available in liquid; easy to apply and touch up	Interior wood in areas not prone to moisture
Tung oil	Produces soft, deep luster, enhancing color and grain; can be thinned and buffed to bright sheen Good resistance to moisture; buffing wax adds protection Good durability; requires periodic reapplication Available in liquid; easy to apply and touch up	Interior wood
SURFACE FINISH		
Shellac	Produces warm, glossy finish, enhancing color (amber hues) and grain Low resistance to moisture and heat Low to fair durability Available in liquid or crystals: white or orange Easy to apply with good results; dries quickly	Interior wood in areas not prone to wear or moisture
Lacquer	Produces hard, glossy finish, intensifying color and grain Excellent resistance to moisture and heat High durability Available in liquid or spray Difficult to apply with good results (spray easiest); dries very quickly	Interior wood in areas prone to wear and moisture: furniture
Varnish	Produces bright, glossy finish, enhancing color (amber hues) and grain Excellent resistance to moisture and heat High durability; does not darken with age or exposure to sunlight Available in liquid Fairly easy to apply with good results; dries slowly, letting dust settle	Interior or exterior wood in areas prone to wear and moisture: floors; staircases; furniture; siding; trim
Polyurethane	Produces warm, satiny or bright, glossy finish, enhancing color and grain Excellent resistance to moisture and heat; virtually waterproof Very high durability; does not darken with age or exposure to sunlight Available in liquid or spray: satin or gloss Easy to apply with good results; dries quickly	Interior or exterior wood in areas prone to wear and moisture: floors; staircases; furniture; siding; trim

PAINTS

TYPE	CHARACTERISTICS	USES
INTERIOR		
Latex	Base of acrylic or polyvinyl resins; available in flat or semi-gloss Odor-free and applies easily; tools cleaned up with water Dries in 2 to 4 hours; durable and washable, but stains easily	Interior wood, drywall, plaster, masonry and metal: primer required for surfaces unfinished or patched
Alkyd	Base of alkyd and other synthetic resins; available in flat, semi-gloss or gloss Little odor and applies sticky; tools cleaned up with mineral spirits Dries in 6 to 8 hours; very durable and washable	Interior wood, drywall, plaster, masonry and metal: primer required for surfaces unfinished or patched; for application of gloss
Texture	Base of acrylic or polyvinyl resins with additives (stiff type of latex); texture hides irregularities and flaws Odor-free and applies easily; tools cleaned up with water Dries in 15 to 30 minutes; durable, but difficult to wash	Interior wood, drywall, plaster or masonry: primer required for surfaces unfinished or patched
EXTERIOR		
Latex	Base of acrylic or vinyl resins and may contain fungicides or mildew-cides; available in flat or semi-gloss Applies easily; tools cleaned up with water Dries in 2 to 4 hours; durable, but stains easily	Exterior wood, masonry and metal: primer required for surfaces unfinished or patched; recommended for coverage of old color
Alkyd	Base of alkyd and other synthetic resins; available in flat, semi-gloss or gloss Applies sticky; tools cleaned up with mineral spirits Dries in 12 to 18 hours (types with drying agents as quickly as 15 minutes to 4 hours); very durable	Exterior wood, masonry and metal: primer required for surfaces unfinished or patched; for application of gloss; recommended for coverage of old color
INTERIOR/EXTERIOR		
Porch, floor or masonry	Base of latex, alkyd, urethane, rubber or epoxy; available in semi-gloss (only rubber-based) or gloss Applies sticky; tools cleaned up with mineral spirits (latex-based with water) Dries in 12 to 18 hours (types with drying agents as quickly as 15 minutes to 4 hours); highly durable and abrasion-resistant	Interior or exterior wood (except rubber-based) and masonry subjected to heavy wear: primer required for surfaces unfinished or patched; for application of alkyd-based
Metal	Base of alkyd or (only primer) latex and may contain rust inhibitor; available in flat (only primer) or gloss Applies easily; tools cleaned up with mineral spirits (latex-based with water) Dries in 6 to 8 hours (latex-based in 2 to 4 hours); very durable	Interior or exterior metal: primer required for application of alkyd-based without rust inhibitor; recommended for coverage of old color

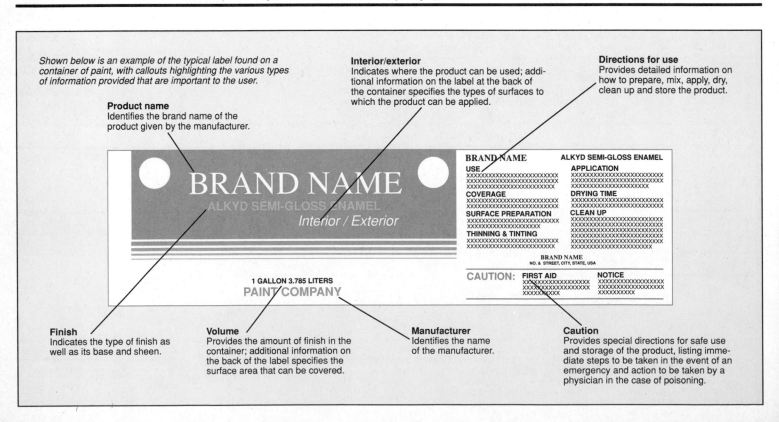

Shown below is an example of the typical label found on a container of paint, with callouts highlighting the various types of information provided that are important to the user.

Product name
Identifies the brand name of the product given by the manufacturer.

Interior/exterior
Indicates where the product can be used; additional information on the label at the back of the container specifies the types of surfaces to which the product can be applied.

Directions for use
Provides detailed information on how to prepare, mix, apply, dry, clean up and store the product.

Finish
Indicates the type of finish as well as its base and sheen.

Volume
Provides the amount of finish in the container; additional information on the back of the label specifies the surface area that can be covered.

Manufacturer
Identifies the name of the manufacturer.

Caution
Provides special directions for safe use and storage of the product, listing immediate steps to be taken in the event of an emergency and action to be taken by a physician in the case of poisoning.

WALLCOVERINGS

TYPE	CHARACTERISTICS	USES
Common paper	Typically with light vinyl coating; may be pre-pasted Susceptible to grease, moisture and abrasion Not scrubbable; washable (dry-cleaning recommended to prevent pattern inks from running) Easy to apply	General applications in low- to moderate-traffic areas prone to light wear and soiling: living rooms; dining rooms; adult bedrooms Not suitable for kitchens; bathrooms
Vinyl	Vinyl laminated to backing of paper or cloth and may be embossed or cork-like; may be pre-pasted Resistant to grease and moisture Washable and scrubbable Most types easy to apply	General applications in high-traffic areas prone to heavy wear and soiling: kitchens; bathrooms; child bedrooms
Foil	Thin aluminum laminated to backing of paper or cloth Not scrubbable; washable Difficult to apply; fragile and tears easily	Decorative highlights: hallways; alcoves
Flocked	Velvet-textured cotton, rayon, nylon or silk on backing of paper, vinyl or foil Not scrubbable; washable (dry-cleaning recommended) Moderately difficult to apply	Decorative highlights and formal areas: hallways; living rooms Not suitable for high-traffic areas
Fabric	Various types available, including cotton or silk Not scrubbable or washable; dry-cleaning only Moderately difficult to apply	Decorative highlights: hallways; living rooms; recreation rooms
Natural fiber	Various types available, including jute, hemp or grasses Not scrubbable or washable; dry-cleaning only	General applications in low- to moderate-traffic areas: living rooms; dining rooms; adult bedrooms
Felt suede	Leather-like appearance; applied over liner Stains easily Not scrubbable or washable; dry-cleaning only Moderately difficult to apply	Decorative highlights and special effects: living rooms; adult bedrooms
Mural	Available in packages of individually-numbered strips: hand-printed types require trimming prior to application; photo-printed types may be pre-pasted Not scrubbable; washable (dry-cleaning recommended to prevent pattern inks from running) Easy to apply	Special effects on focal walls: living rooms; adult bedrooms
Liner	Plain pulp paper available in light, medium or heavy weight Provides uniform, porous base for wallcovering adhesive Easy to apply	Prior to application of hand-printed or felt/suede wallcovering on drywall, plaster, paneling (other than tongue-and-groove) or masonry

ROPES AND CORDS

TYPE	CHARACTERISTICS	USES
NATURAL FIBER		
Manila	Made from abaca plant; strongest natural-fiber type Stretches only slightly under load; easy to tie	General applications where strength important
Sisal	Made from agabe sisala plant; not as strong as manila type Stretches moderately under load; easy to tie	Moderate-weight applications
Jute	Made from jute plant; not as strong as sisal type Stretches moderately under load; easy to tie	Light- to moderate-weight applications
Cotton	Made from 100% cotton or cotton blended with polyester; not as strong as jute type Stretches under load; easy to tie	Light-weight applications: clotheslines
SYNTHETIC FIBER		
Nylon	Strongest synthetic-fiber type Solid braid or twisted; twisted type prone to unraveling when cut Stretches under load; easy to tie	Applications where sudden load would snap another type: hoisting; towing
Polyester	Almost as strong as nylon type and more durable Stretches only slightly under load; easy to tie	General applications where strength and withstanding weather important
Polypropylene	Not as strong as polyester type, but stronger than natural-fiber types Deteriorates quickly, but floats on water; difficult to tie	Applications on water: pool lifelines; markers

PIPE FITTINGS

SUPPLY PIPE FITTINGS

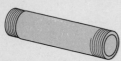

Nipple
Joins threaded fittings positioned close together; often used to complete run of threaded pipe.

Tee
Joins straight run and 90° branch run of threaded pipes.

Street elbow
Connected to another fitting to change direction of threaded pipe.

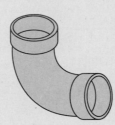

Elbow
Changes direction of unthreaded pipe; available in bends of 45° and 90°.

Coupling
Joins unthreaded pipes of straight run: pipe ends bottom out against shoulder inside standard coupling; slip coupling has no shoulder.

Union
Joins threaded pipes of straight run; permits run to be disassembled.

Plug
Closes unused opening in threaded fitting; can be used to temporarily plug opening in threaded fitting if water must be turned on during repair.

DRAINPIPE FITTINGS

Quarter bend (90° elbow)
Changes direction of drainpipe of cast iron, polyvinyl chloride (PVC) or acrylonitrile butadiene styrene (ABS).

Hub
Joins drainpipes of cast iron, polyvinyl chloride (PVC) or acrylonitrile butadiene styrene (ABS): hub-and-spigot joints of old pipes of cast iron sealed with oakum and lead; joints of pipes of plastic commonly called couplings.

Hubless fitting
Joins hubless drainpipes of cast iron, polyvinyl chloride (PVC) or acrylonitrile butadiene styrene (ABS) without caulking or cement; tight-fitting sleeve of neoprene rubber held in place over joint by collar and clamps of stainless steel.

Sanitary wye with cleanout
Joins straight run of drainpipes; threaded cleanout plug allows access to run of drainpipe for cleaning and augering.

Reducer
Joins straight run of drainpipes of different diameters.

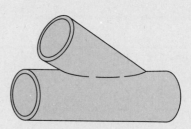

Wye branch
Joins straight run and 45° branch run of drainpipes.

TRANSITION FITTINGS

Dielectric union
Joins pipes of copper and galvanized steel to prevent electrolytic corrosion between different metals: threaded end screwed to pipe of galvanized steel; brass end sweat-soldered to pipe of copper.

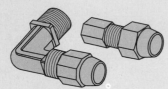

Threaded adapters
Joins pipe of copper, polybutylene (PB) or chlorinated polyvinyl chloride (CPVC) to threaded pipe; different types for cold- and hot-water supply pipes.

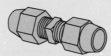

Compression fitting
Joins pipes of copper, polybutylene (PB) or chlorinated polyvinyl chloride (CPVC) without solder or solvent cement.

CPVC-to-unthreaded pipe adapter
Compression end clamped to pipe of copper or polybutylene (PB); socket end connected to pipe of chlorinated polyvinyl chloride (CPVC) with solvent cement.

CPVC-to-threaded pipe adapter
Threaded end screwed to pipe of galvanized steel or brass; socket end connected to pipe of chlorinated polyvinyl chloride (CPVC) with solvent cement.

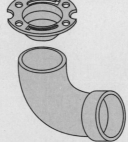

Closet flange and bend
Connects toilet to branch run of drainpipes; helps anchor it to bathroom floor.

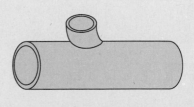

Reducing tee-wye
Joins straight run and 90° branch run of drainpipes; branch run of smaller diameter.

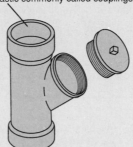

PIPES

TYPE	CHARACTERISTICS	USES
METAL		
Brass	Threaded: connected with screw-on fittings Available in lengths of 12 feet Easy to handle and cut; does not bend	Supply pipes (nipples and extensions)
Copper	Unthreaded: connected with sweat-soldered, compression or screw-on fittings Available in rigid lengths of 10 or 20 feet and flexible coils of up to 60 feet: medium-thick Type L (color-coded green); thin-walled Type M (color-coded red) Easy to handle and cut; Type M bends	Supply pipes
Galvanized steel	Threaded: connected with screw-on fittings Typically available in lengths of 21 feet Difficult to handle and cut; does not bend Stronger than copper or brass; prone to corrosion	Supply pipes (especially if unprotected or exposed to vibration)
Cast iron	Unthreaded: connected with hub-and-spigot joints or hubless fittings Typically available in lengths of 5 feet Difficult to handle and cut; does not bend	Drainpipes; vents
PLASTIC		
Polybutylene (PB)	Unthreaded: connected with compression fittings Available in coils of up to 1000 feet Easy to handle and cut; bends	Supply pipes (especially long runs around beams and corners or behind walls)
Chlorinated polyvinyl chloride (CPVC)	Unthreaded: connected with solvent cement Typically available in lengths of 10 feet Easy to handle and cut; does not bend	Supply pipes
Polyvinyl chloride (PVC)	Unthreaded: connected with solvent cement or hubless fittings Available in lengths of 10 or 20 feet Easy to handle and cut; does not bend	Drainpipes
Acrylonitrile butadiene styrene (ABS)	Unthreaded: connected with solvent cement or hubless fittings Available in lengths of 10 or 20 feet Easy to handle and cut; does not bend	Drainpipes

PIPE DIMENSIONS

TYPE	OUTSIDE DIAMETER (OD) (INCHES)	INSIDE DIAMETER (ID) (INCHES)	DEPTH OF FITTING SOCKET (INCHES)
Brass or galvanized steel (threaded)	3/8	1/8	1/4
	1/2	1/4	3/8
	5/8	3/8	3/8
	3/4	1/2	1/2
	1	3/4	9/16
	1 1/4	1	11/16
	1 1/2	1 1/4	11/16
	1 3/4	1 1/2	11/16
	2 1/4	2	3/4
Copper (unthreaded)	3/8	1/4	5/16
	1/2	3/8	3/8
	5/8	1/2	1/2
	7/8	3/4	3/4
	1 1/8	1	15/16
	1 3/8	1 1/4	1
	1 5/8	1 1/2	1 1/8

TYPE	OUTSIDE DIAMETER (OD) (INCHES)	INSIDE DIAMETER (ID) (INCHES)	DEPTH OF FITTING SOCKET (INCHES)
Plastic (unthreaded)	7/8	1/2	1/2
	1 1/8	3/4	5/8
	1 3/8	1	3/4
	1 5/8	1 1/4	11/16
	1 7/8	1 1/2	11/16
	2 3/8	2	3/4
	3 3/8	3	1 1/2
	4 3/8	4	1 3/4
Cast iron (unthreaded)	2 1/4	2	2 1/2
	3 1/4	3	2 3/4
	4 1/4	4	3
	5 1/4	5	3
	6 1/4	6	3

Reading the chart. Use replacement pipe of the same inside diameter (ID) as the old pipe. When you cut replacement pipe, be sure to account for the depth of the sockets for its fittings.

FUSES

TYPE	CHARACTERISTICS	USES
Low-voltage fuse	Available in ratings of up to 20 amperes to suit gauge of wire in circuit Signals short circuit or overloaded circuit	Appliances; entertainment units
Standard plug fuse	Available in ratings of 15, 20 or 30 amperes to suit gauge of wire in circuit Signals short circuit or overloaded circuit	Fuse-type service panels: circuits of standard light fixtures and small appliances
Time-delay fuse	Available in ratings of 15, 20 or 30 amperes to suit gauge of wire in circuit Withstands momentary power surge in circuit due to motor start-up; signals short circuit or sustained, overloaded circuit	Fuse-type service panels: circuits of power-demanding, motorized small appliances
Type-S fuse	Available in ratings of 15, 20 or 30 amperes to suit gauge of wire in circuit Fuse fits adapter screwed into service panel; adapter accepts only Type-S fuse of matching amperage Signals short circuit or overloaded circuit	Fuse-type service panels: circuits of standard light fixtures and small appliances to guard against accidental installation of fuse with higher amperage rating
Ferrule-type cartridge fuse	Available in ratings of up to 60 amperes to suit gauge of wire in circuit Withstands momentary power surge in circuit; signals short circuit or sustained, overloaded circuit	Fuse-type service panels: circuits of power-demanding, motorized major appliances
Knife-blade cartridge fuse	Available in ratings of more than 60 amperes to protect electrical system of household Withstands momentary power surge in electrical system; signals short circuit or sustained, overloaded circuit	Fuse-type service panels: main fuse block

BLOWN FUSES

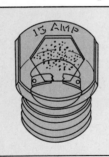

Short circuit. A short circuit rapidly vaporizes the center of the metal strip, discoloring the window.

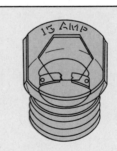

Overloaded circuit. An overloaded circuit slowly melts the center of the metal strip, leaving the window unchanged.

WIRE AMPERAGE CAPACITY

WIRE	GAUGE	AMPERES	WIRE	GAUGE	AMPERES
Copper wire	No. 20	5	Aluminum wire	No. 12	15
	No. 18	7		No. 10	20
	No. 16	10		No. 8	30
	No. 14	15		No. 6	40
	No. 12	20		No. 4	60
	No. 10	30		No. 3	70
	No. 8	40		No. 2	80
	No. 6	55		No. 1	90
	No. 4	70		No. 0	100

WIRES AND CABLES

TYPE	CHARACTERISTICS	USES
Grounding wire	One solid No. 10 copper wire Sometimes covered with insulation	Entertainment units: grounding connection of turntable to receiver
Single-conductor wire (bell wire)	One stranded or solid No. 16 or No. 18 wire; covered with insulation of plastic Solid type without insulation called bus wire	Doorbells; entertainment units; small appliances
Two-conductor cable (speaker cable or zip cord)	Two stranded or solid No. 16 or No. 18 wires; covered with insulation of plastic Insulation of neutral wire usually marked by molded ridge to help prevent reversing polarity	Entertainment units: connecting of speakers to receiver; small appliances; table lamps
Multi-conductor cable	Three to five insulated, stranded or solid No. 16 or No. 18 wires; covered with sheathing of plastic, rubber or heat-resistant material Insulation of wires usually color-coded or otherwise marked to help prevent reversing polarity	Entertainment units; small appliances
Two-conductor cable with grounding wire	Two insulated, stranded or solid wires: black (hot) and white (neutral); bare copper wire for grounding Covered with sheathing of plastic, rubber or heat-resistant material	General wiring of household circuits
Three-conductor cable with grounding wire	Three insulated, stranded or solid wires: black, red (both hot) and white (neutral); bare copper wire for grounding Covered with sheathing of plastic, rubber or heat-resistant material	General wiring of household circuits: three- or four-way switches; split-circuit outlets
Shielded one-conductor cable (patch cord)	One insulated, solid or stranded wire; spiral or braided shield acts as ground and protects insulated wire from interference Covered with sheathing of plastic, rubber or heat-resistant material	Entertainment units; small appliances
Shielded two-conductor cable	Two insulated, solid or stranded wires; spiral or braided shield acts as ground and protects insulated wires from interference Covered with sheathing of plastic, rubber or heat-resistant material	Entertainment units; small appliances
Flat twin-lead cable	Two stranded wires; covered with sheathing of plastic Susceptible to interference	Entertainment units: connecting of receiver to indoor FM antenna
Shielded twin-lead cable	Two stranded wires; covered with insulation of foam and sheathing of plastic May contain inner shield of foil to protect insulated wires from interference	Entertainment units: connecting of television to antenna
Coaxial cable	One solid or stranded wire covered with insulation of foam; spiral or braided shield acts as ground and protects insulated wires from interference Covered with sheathing of plastic, rubber or heat-resistant material	Entertainment units: connecting of videocassette recorder to television
Telephone cable	Four insulated, solid or stranded wires; covered with sheathing of plastic Insulation of wires color-coded to help prevent reversing polarity: black, red, green and yellow	Telephone equipment
Ribbon cable	Multiple solid wires; covered with insulation of plastic Ribbon cable connectors pierce insulation to contact wires	Computer equipment: connecting of main unit to printer
Armored cable	Two wires and metal bonding strip or grounding wire; wrapped in paper and sheathed in flexible steel Often found in older homes	General wiring of household circuits
Service cable	Typically No. 1/0 to 4/0 cable	Carries electricity from power lines of utility company to main service panel of household electrical system

WIRE AND CABLE MARKINGS

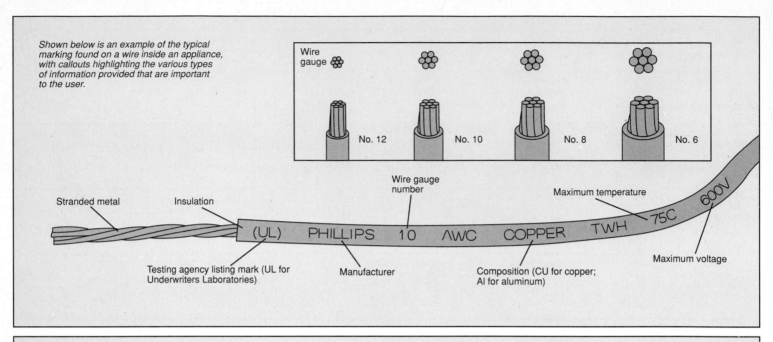

Shown below is an example of the typical marking found on a wire inside an appliance, with callouts highlighting the various types of information provided that are important to the user.

Wire gauge

No. 12   No. 10   No. 8   No. 6

Wire gauge number

Maximum temperature

600V

Stranded metal   Insulation

(UL)   PHILLIPS   10   AWC   COPPER   TWH   75C

Maximum voltage

Testing agency listing mark (UL for Underwriters Laboratories)

Manufacturer

Composition (CU for copper; Al for aluminum)

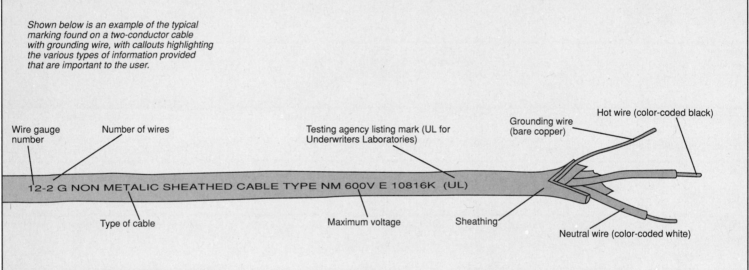

Shown below is an example of the typical marking found on a two-conductor cable with grounding wire, with callouts highlighting the various types of information provided that are important to the user.

Wire gauge number

Number of wires

Testing agency listing mark (UL for Underwriters Laboratories)

Grounding wire (bare copper)

Hot wire (color-coded black)

12-2 G NON METALIC SHEATHED CABLE TYPE NM 600V E 10816K (UL)

Type of cable   Maximum voltage   Sheathing

Neutral wire (color-coded white)

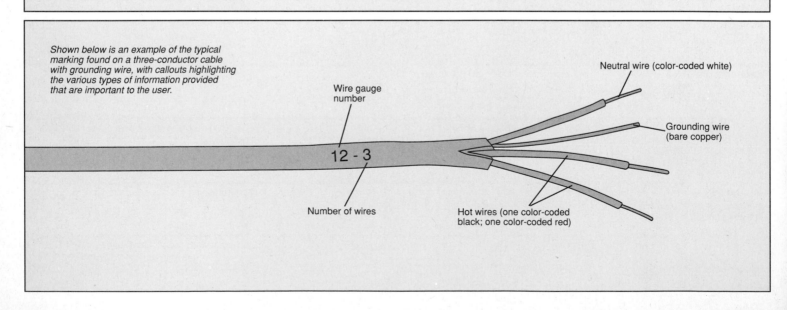

Shown below is an example of the typical marking found on a three-conductor cable with grounding wire, with callouts highlighting the various types of information provided that are important to the user.

Neutral wire (color-coded white)

Wire gauge number

Grounding wire (bare copper)

12 - 3

Number of wires

Hot wires (one color-coded black; one color-coded red)

120-VOLT OUTLETS

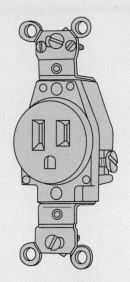

Standard single outlet
Accommodates only one lamp or appliance; commonly found in older homes.

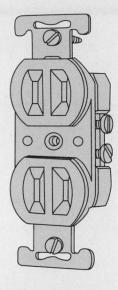

Two-slot duplex outlet
Does not provide grounding and cannot accommodate three-prong plugs; commonly found in older homes and not for use in new installations.

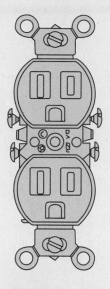

Standard grounded duplex outlet
Provides grounding; accommodates three-prong plugs: long (neutral) slot for wide prong; shorter (hot) slot for narrow prong; grounding slot for grounding prong.

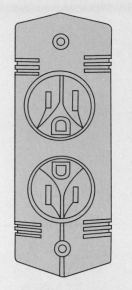

Surface-mounted duplex outlet
Has removable front cover; typically found on baseboards of older homes.

Clock hanger outlet
Recessed single-receptacle outlet with hook; allows appliance or fixture to hang flush against wall.

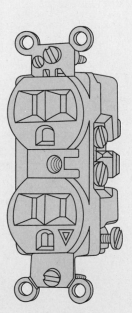

Duplex outlet with isolated ground
Insulated grounding terminal cuts down on electrical interference; inverted triangle denotes isolated ground.

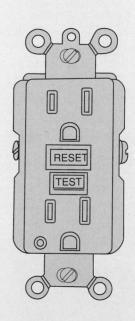

GFCI-protected duplex outlet
Provides grounding protected by GFCI (ground-fault circuit interrupter); accommodates three-prong plugs: long (neutral) slot for wide prong; shorter (hot) slot for narrow prong; grounding slot for grounding prong. Trips instantly if leak in electrical current to ground detected.

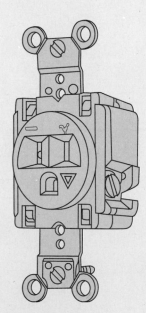

Single outlet with surge suppressor
Provides protection against surges of electrical current; inverted triangle denotes isolated ground.

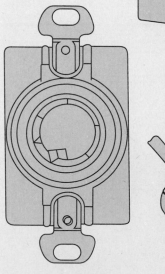

Twist-lock 20-amp outlet
Heavy-duty outlet with locking action to secure connection of power cord.

WALL SWITCHES

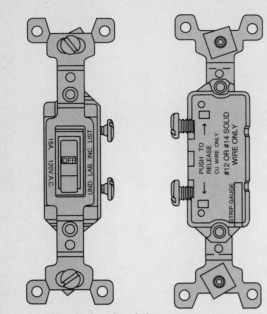

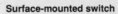

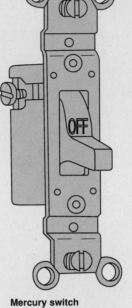

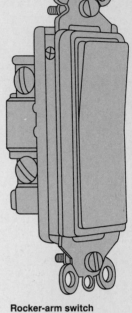

Standard single-pole switch
Typically has two screw terminals; may have push-in terminals or wire leads. May have grounding screw terminal color-coded green or marked GR. Automatic timer (heat-, sound- or motion-activated) models available. Multiple-pole types also available: three-way (three terminals); four-way (four terminals). For most general applications.

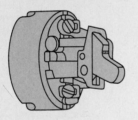

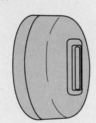

Locking switch
Typically single-pole (two terminals). Requires special key inserted into slot of face to operate; small metal objects inserted into keyhole do not contact electrical parts. For special applications where restricted access for safety important: workshop; garage.

Surface-mounted switch
Typically single-pole (two terminals); wires enter side of housing and connect to screw terminals inside it. Cover can be pried off by inserting screwdriver into slot on side and turning it. Commonly found in older homes: utility room; garage.

Mercury switch
May be single-pole (two terminals), three-way (three terminals) or four-way (four terminals). Has few moving parts; when toggle set to ON, pool of mercury bridges two contacts inside sealed drum. Top of mounting strap marked TOP to ensure correct installation. Not recommended except for special applications where long, quiet operation important.

Rocker-arm switch
May be single-pole (two terminals), three-way (three terminals) or four-way (four terminals); large toggle that may have pilot light. Relatively expensive. For general applications, especially in areas where hands may be full and operation of switch by elbow would be important: laundry room; staircase or hallway.

LIGHT SOCKETS

Medium-base lamp socket
Normally of metal, but can be of plastic; may contain simple ON/OFF switch or three-way switch. Typically found in floor or table lamps; some chandeliers.

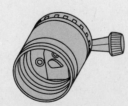

Plastic fixture socket
Attached to fixture with external mounting strap. Model shown has preattached wires.

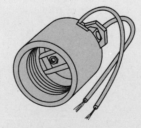

Low-voltage socket
Small-based socket designed to receive low-voltage bulbs. Model shown has bayonet base with preattached wires; may have threaded metal base.

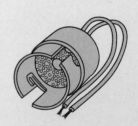

Porcelain fixture socket
Attached to fixture with internal mounting screw. Model shown has one brass terminal screw and one silver terminal screw.

Two-part socket
Separates into two parts that fit into socket hole from each side and screw together; provides for easy installation.

Outdoor socket
Exterior-grade socket of porcelain; may be of plastic or rubber. Model shown has external mounting tabs.

LIGHT BULBS

TYPE		CHARACTERISTICS	USES
A-type		Most common type of light bulb Indoor and weather-resistant types available Fits medium-base socket Range of wattages from 4 watts to 300 watts	Standard lamps and fixtures
Three-way		Provides low, medium and high light-intensities Fits three-way socket Range of wattages includes 30/70/100 watts, 40/60/100 watts and 100/200/300 watts	Lamps with three-way sockets
Long-life		Filaments burn at low temperature; up to three times life of standard A-type bulb Fits medium-base socket Range of wattages from 40 watts to 150 watts	General applications where long-lasting bulb important: stairways; hallways; hard-to-reach fixtures
T (tubular)		Fits medium-base socket Range of wattages from 15 watts to 150 watts	Medium light-intensity desk lamps; showcase applications: fixture above picture; canopy of aquarium
Candelabra		Fits medium-base or candelabra socket Range of wattages from 15 watts to 60 watts	Lamps and fixtures where low light-intensity or accent lighting desired
G (globe)		Decorative bulb; does not require shade Fits medium-base or candelabra socket Range of wattages from 40 watts to 150 watts	Fixtures around makeup mirrors; hanging fixtures
Night light		Small, low-wattage bulb Fits medium-base or candelabra socket Range of wattages includes 4 watts, 7 watts and 7 1/2 watts	Plug-in fixtures to illuminate hallways or other areas at night; Christmas lights
R (reflector) (spotlight)		Built-in reflector directs beam Fits medium-base socket Range of wattages from 15 watts to 60 watts	Adjustable fixtures where directional lighting required: track lighting
PAR (parabolic aluminized reflector) (floodlight)		Bright, high-wattage bulb Fits medium-base socket Range of wattages from 25 watts to 250 watts	Recessed fixtures; track lighting; outdoor fixtures
ER (ellipsoidal reflector)		Fits medium-base socket Range of wattages from 50 watts to 120 watts	Recessed downlight fixtures
Low-voltage		Requires transformer to reduce 120-volt electrical current of household Fits medium-base, candelabra or bayonet socket Range of voltage ratings from 6 volts to 16 volts	Indoor fixtures; temporary outdoor fixtures

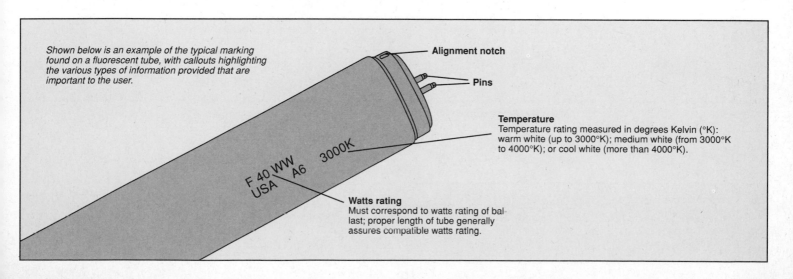

Shown below is an example of the typical marking found on a fluorescent tube, with callouts highlighting the various types of information provided that are important to the user.

Alignment notch

Pins

F 40 WW A6
USA 3000K

Temperature
Temperature rating measured in degrees Kelvin (°K):
warm white (up to 3000°K); medium white (from 3000°K
to 4000°K); or cool white (more than 4000°K).

Watts rating
Must correspond to watts rating of ballast; proper length of tube generally assures compatible watts rating.

WEATHER STRIPPING

TYPE	CHARACTERISTICS	USES
Metal strip	Provides sliding seal Nailed to jamb against exterior of door or window sash Long-lasting; may dent or loosen from nails and bend	Exterior doors Garage doors Windows
Wood strip	Provides pressure seal Nailed to jamb against exterior of door or window sash Long-lasting	Exterior doors Double-hung windows (wood sashes)
Open-cell foam strip	Provides pressure seal Positioned along closing side of doorstop or bottom of window sash; self-adhesive, but may be nailed or stapled Wears out quickly and deforms easily, losing shape; seasonal replacement recommended	Interior doors Double-hung windows (wood sashes)
Closed-cell foam strip	Provides pressure seal; good for slightly uneven gaps Positioned along doorstop or stop or bottom of window sash; self-adhesive, but may be nailed or stapled Long-lasting, retaining shape and flexibility; loosens and wears quickly on sliding surfaces	Exterior doors Hinged windows
V strip	Provides sliding seal; plastic type also pressure seal Metal type nailed; plastic type self-adhesive Long-lasting; may dent or loosen and bend	Exterior doors Windows
Spring-loaded jamb strip	Provides pressure seal Screwed to jamb through attachment strip; caulking behind attachment strip improves seal Long-lasting	Exterior doors Hinged windows
Magnetic jamb strip	Provides pressure seal Screwed to jamb (with steel strip for wood) through attachment strip; factory-installed on prehung doors and windows Long-lasting; seal may deteriorate in extreme cold	Exterior doors Hinged windows
Pile strip	Provides sliding seal Self-adhesive, snap-in or installed with splining tool; factory-installed on window sashes of metal Moderately long-lasting; plastic film insert on some types improves seal	Windows (metal sashes)
Rubber strip	Provides pressure seal Nailed to bottom of door Long-lasting	Garage doors
Tubular gasket	Provides pressure seal; good for irregular gaps Positioned along doorstop or stop or bottom of window sash; self-adhesive, but may be nailed or stapled Long-lasting, retaining shape; plastic type less flexible and resistant to cold than rubber type	Exterior doors Windows
Partial threshold	Provides pressure seal Nailed or screwed to door sill through metal plate Long-lasting; rubber or plastic insert may wear out quickly, but can be replaced	Exterior doors without threshold (storm doors)

TYPE	CHARACTERISTICS	USES
Complete threshold	Provides sliding and pressure seal; replaces worn threshold of wood Screwed to door sill through metal plate; door may need to be trimmed Long-lasting; rubber or plastic insert may wear out quickly, but can be replaced	Exterior doors
Grooved gasket	Provides pressure seal; usually made-to-measure Snaps over metal or glass slat edges of window; may be secured with special adhesive Long-lasting, retaining shape	Casement, jalousie and some multi-vent awning windows (metal sashes)
Door sweep	Provides sliding and pressure seal; may drag on carpeting Screwed to bottom on interior of door Moderately long-lasting; rubber, plastic or pile insert may wear out quickly, but can be replaced	Exterior doors
Door shoe	Provides sliding seal; available in several styles Screwed to bottom on interior and exterior of door through attachment strips; door may need to be trimmed Long-lasting; rubber, plastic or pile insert may wear out quickly, but can be replaced	Exterior doors

INSULATION

TYPE	CHARACTERISTICS	USES
Vermiculite (expanded mica)	Approximate R-value of 2.08 per inch of thickness Available in loose-fill form Does not irritate skin Fire-resistant; absorbs moisture	Hollow spaces
Perlite	Approximate R-value of 2.7 per inch of thickness Available in loose-fill form; can be poured Does not irritate skin Fire-resistant; absorbs moisture	Hollow spaces
Fiberglass	Approximate R-value of 3.33 per inch of thickness Available in loose-fill, batt or blanket form Particles can irritate skin Fire-resistant; gives off odor when damp	General applications for walls, ceilings and floors; attic floors; dormer walls and ceilings; basements and crawlspaces; overhangs; unheated garages
Rock wool	Approximate R-value of 3.33 per inch of thickness Available in loose-fill, batt or blanket form Particles can irritate skin Fire-resistant	General applications for walls, ceilings and floors; attic floors; dormer walls and ceilings; basements and crawlspaces; overhangs; unheated garages
Polystyrene	Approximate R-value of 3.45 per inch of thickness Available in rigid-board or bead form Does not irritate skin Combustible; moisture-resistant	Foundation walls; below-grade floors
Cellulose	Approximate R-value of 3.7 per inch of thickness Available in loose-fill, batt or blanket form Does not irritate skin Flammable unless chemically treated	General applications for walls, ceilings and floors; attic floors; dormer walls and ceilings; basements and crawlspaces; overhangs; unheated garages Loose-fill form in hollow spaces
Urethane	Approximate R-value of 5.3 per inch of thickness Available professionally foamed-in-place Combustible; gives off noxious fumes if ignited	General applications for walls, ceilings and floors; attic floors; dormer walls and ceilings; basements and crawlspaces; overhangs; unheated garages

CLEANING AGENTS

TYPE	CHARACTERISTICS	USES
Abrasive cleaner	Powder or liquid form under many brand names Available at supermarket	Removing stains from most durable surfaces
All-purpose cleaner	Powder, liquid or spray form under many brand names Available at supermarket	General, light to heavy cleaning of most surfaces
Acetone	Liquid form Available at building supply center	Cleaning up spills of epoxy glue; plastic laminate filler; flammable, solvent-based contact cement
Ammonia	Liquid form; type containing ammonium hydroxide in 2% to 3% solution recommended Available at supermarket	Heavy cleaning of most durable surfaces: glass
Ammonium sulfamate (herbicide)	Powder form Available at garden supply center	Removing organic stains from wood or masonry
Benzene (and thickener)	Liquid form Available at building supply center	Removing oil, grease or tar from stone
Carpet cleaner	Powder form Available at supermarket or carpeting supply center	Removing food or beverage stains from carpeting
Ceramic-tile stripper	Liquid form; water-based type recommended Available at building supply center	Removing stains from ceramic
Chlorine bleach (laundry bleach)	Liquid form under many brand names; type containing sodium hypochlorite in 5% to 6% solution recommended Available at supermarket	Removing mildew from most durable surfaces
Citrus-based solvent	Liquid form; type containing D-limonene in 86% to 90% solution recommended Available at janitorial or chemical supply center	Removing stains from most durable surfaces
Contact cement cleaner or thinner	Liquid form Available at building supply center	Cleaning up spills of contact cement
Cornstarch	Powder form Available at supermarket	Removing stains from light-colored marble
Degreaser	Liquid form under many brand names Available at janitorial or chemical supply center	Removing greasy or oily stains from most durable surfaces
Denatured alcohol	Liquid form Available at building supply center	Cleaning up spills of epoxy glue; shellac
Dishwashing liquid	Liquid form under many brand names Available at supermarket	General, light cleaning of most surfaces
Dry-cleaning fluid	Liquid form under many brand and chemical names; type containing chlorinated hydrocarbon (1-1-1 trichloroethane or perchloroethane) most common Available at janitorial or chemical supply center	Removing stains from most non-washable or delicate surfaces
Hydrogen peroxide	Liquid form; type containing peroxide of hydrogen in 3% solution recommended Available at drugstore	Removing stains from delicate surfaces
Lacquer thinner	Liquid form Available at building supply center	Cleaning up spills of lacquer; shellac
Laundry detergent	Powder form under many brand names; enzyme type identified on label Available at supermarket	General, light to heavy cleaning of most surfaces Enzyme type for removing stains from delicate surfaces
Lemon juice	Liquid form; citric acid in 3% to 5% solution Available at supermarket	Removing stains fom delicate surfaces
Marble-floor polish stripper	Liquid form; solvent-based type recommended Available at building or flooring supply center	Removing stains from marble
Mineral spirits	Liquid form Available at building supply center	Removing stains from wood
Muriatic acid	Liquid form Available at building supply center	Removing efflorescence from masonry
Oxalic acid	Powder form; pure type recommended Available at janitorial or chemical supply center	Removing rust stains from wood or masonry
Oxygen bleach	Powder form under many chemical names; type containing sodium perborate or sodium borate recommended Available at janitorial or chemical supply center	Removing mildew from wood or masonry

TYPE	CHARACTERISTICS	USES
Phosphoric acid	Liquid form; type in 75% to 85% solution recommended Available at janitorial or chemical supply center	Removing efflorescence or rust from masonry
Rubbing alcohol (isopropyl alcohol)	Liquid form Available at drugstore	Removing stains from most durable surfaces
Scouring powder	Powder form under many brand names Available at supermarket	Removing stains from most durable surfaces
Sodium bicarbonate (baking soda)	Powder form Available at supermarket	Removing stains from delicate surfaces; neutralizing acids
Sodium metasilicate (truck wash)	Powder form; pure type recommended Available at automotive, janitorial or chemical supply center	Removing organic stains from wood or masonry
Trisodium phosphate (TSP)	Powder form Available at drugstore	Heavy cleaning of most durable surfaces
Turpentine	Liquid form Available at building supply center	Cleaning up spills of oil-based finish
White vinegar	Liquid form; type containing acetic acid in 4% to 8% solution recommended Available at supermarket	General, light cleaning of most durable surfaces: glass
Wood bleach	Liquid form Available at building supply center	Removing deep stains from wood
Wood floor cleaner	Liquid form Available at building supply or flooring center	Removing superficial stains from wood

PESTICIDES

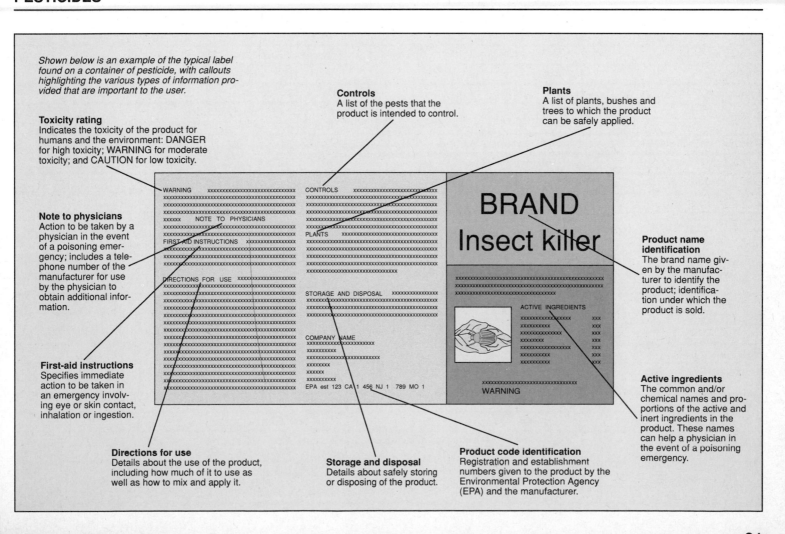

Shown below is an example of the typical label found on a container of pesticide, with callouts highlighting the various types of information provided that are important to the user.

Controls
A list of the pests that the product is intended to control.

Plants
A list of plants, bushes and trees to which the product can be safely applied.

Toxicity rating
Indicates the toxicity of the product for humans and the environment: DANGER for high toxicity; WARNING for moderate toxicity; and CAUTION for low toxicity.

Note to physicians
Action to be taken by a physician in the event of a poisoning emergency; includes a telephone number of the manufacturer for use by the physician to obtain additional information.

First-aid instructions
Specifies immediate action to be taken in an emergency involving eye or skin contact, inhalation or ingestion.

Product name identification
The brand name given by the manufacturer to identify the product; identification under which the product is sold.

Active ingredients
The common and/or chemical names and proportions of the active and inert ingredients in the product. These names can help a physician in the event of a poisoning emergency.

Directions for use
Details about the use of the product, including how much of it to use as well as how to mix and apply it.

Storage and disposal
Details about safely storing or disposing of the product.

Product code identification
Registration and establishment numbers given to the product by the Environmental Protection Agency (EPA) and the manufacturer.

BRAND
Insect killer

PESTICIDES (continued)

TYPE (ACTIVE INGREDIENT)	CHARACTERISTICS	USES
Acephate	Liquid form; low toxicity	Outdoors: lawn and garden insect pests
Allethrin	Aerosol or liquid form; low toxicity	Indoors: stored-food insect pests; outdoors: biting flies
Avermectin	Poison-bait form; low toxicity	Indoors: cockroaches
Bacillus popilliae (Bp)	Liquid form; no toxicity	Outdoors: beetles
Bacillus thuringiensis (Bt)	Liquid form; no toxicity	Outdoors: caterpillars, moths
Bendiocarb	Dust or wettable-powder form; moderate toxicity	Indoors: cockroaches, fabric insect pests, firebrats, silverfish, stored-food insect pests; outdoors: ants, fleas, spiders, wasps
Bioallethrin (d-trans-allethrin)	Aerosol or liquid form; low toxicity	Indoors: bedbugs; outdoors: biting flies
Boric acid	Dust form; low toxicity	Indoors: bedbugs, cockroaches, firebrats, silverfish; outdoors: ants
Carbaryl	Dust, wettable-powder, granular or poison-bait form; low toxicity	Indoors: cockroaches, firebrats, silverfish; infested pets (non-bait form): fleas, ticks; outdoors: lawn and garden insect pests, wasps
Chlorpyrifos	Liquid, dust, granular or poison-bait form; moderate toxicity	Indoors: cockroaches, fabric insect pests, firebrats, silverfish, stored-food insect pests; outdoors: biting flies, fleas, lawn and garden insect pests, spiders, ticks, wasps
Cyfluthrin	Aerosol or wettable-powder form; moderate toxicity	Indoors: cockroaches, firebrats, silverfish, ticks
Cypermethrin	Liquid or wettable-powder form; moderate toxicity	Indoors: cockroaches, firebrats, silverfish, ticks; outdoors: ants
DEET	Aerosol or liquid form; low toxicity	Repellent: biting flies, chiggers, ticks (**Caution:** Use product containing no more than 15% DEET for child under 7 years of age)
Diatomaceous earth	Dust form; no toxicity	Indoors: bedbugs; outdoors: fleas, lawn and garden insect pests
Diazinon	Liquid, dust, wettable-powder or granular form; low to moderate toxicity	Indoors: cockroaches, fabric insect pests, firebrats, silverfish, stored-food insect pests; outdoors: ants, biting flies, fleas, lawn and garden insect pests, spiders, ticks, wasps
Dichlorvos (DDVP)	Aerosol or pest-strip form; high toxicity	Outdoors: biting flies
Dimethoate	Liquid form; moderate toxicity	Outdoors: lawn and garden insect pests
Disulfoton	Granular or insecticidal-stick form; high toxicity	Indoors: plant insect pests
D-limonene	Aerosol or liquid form; low to moderate toxicity	Infested pets: fleas, ticks
Fenoxycarb	Aerosol or liquid form; low toxicity	Indoors: cockroaches, firebrats, fleas, silverfish; outdoors: ants
Fenvalerate	Aerosol or liquid form; low to moderate toxicity	Indoors: cockroaches, firebrats, silverfish, stored-food insect pests, ticks; outdoors: ants, chiggers, spiders
Horticultural oil (dormant)	Liquid form; low toxicity	Outdoors: lawn and garden insect pests
Hydramethylnon	Poison-bait form; low toxicity	Indoors: cockroaches, firebrats, silverfish; outdoors: ants
Hydroprene	Aerosol or liquid form; low toxicity	Indoors: cockroaches, firebrats, silverfish
Insecticidal soap	Liquid form; no toxicity	Indoors: plant insect pests; outdoors: lawn and garden insect pests
Malathion	Liquid, dust, wettable-powder or poison-bait form; low toxicity	Indoors: cockroaches, fabric insect pests, firebrats, fleas, plant insect pests, stored-food insect pests, ticks; outdoors: ants, biting flies, lawn and garden insect pests, spiders, wasps
Metaldehyde	Poison-bait form; low toxicity	Outdoors: lawn and garden insect pests
Methiocarb	Poison-bait form; moderate toxicity	Outdoors: lawn and garden insect pests
Methoprene	Aerosol form; low toxicity	Indoors: fleas; outdoors: ants
Methoxychlor	Aerosol, liquid, dust or wettable-powder form; low toxicity	Outdoors: lawn and garden insect pests
Nosema locustae	Liquid form; no toxicity	Outdoors: grasshoppers, mole crickets
Permethrin	Aerosol, liquid or wettable-powder form; low toxicity	Indoors: cockroaches, fabric insect pests, firebrats, fleas, silverfish, ticks; outdoors: ants
Phenothrin	Aerosol form; low toxicity	Outdoors: biting flies
Propetamphos	Liquid form; low toxicity	Outdoors: spiders
Propoxur	Aerosol, liquid or poison-bait form; moderate toxicity	Indoors: cockroaches, fabric insect pests, firebrats, fleas, silverfish, ticks; outdoors: biting flies, lawn and garden pests, spiders, wasps
Pyrethrins	Aerosol, liquid or dust form; low toxicity	Indoors: bedbugs, cockroaches, fabric insect pests, fleas, firebrats, plant insect pests, silverfish, stored-food insect pests, ticks; outdoors: biting flies, lawn and garden insect pests, spiders, wasps

TYPE (ACTIVE INGREDIENT)	CHARACTERISTICS	USES
Resmethrin	Aerosol or liquid form; low toxicity	Indoors: plant insect pests; infested pets: fleas, ticks; outdoors: ants, biting flies, lawn and garden insect pests, spiders, wasps
Rotenone	Aerosol, liquid or dust form; moderate toxicity	Outdoors: lawn and garden insect pests
Ryania	Dust form; low toxicity	Outdoors: lawn and garden insect pests
Sabadilla	Dust form; moderate toxicity	Outdoors: lawn and garden insect pests
Silica gel or aerogel	Dust form; low toxicity	Indoors: bedbugs, cockroaches, firebrats, silverfish
Sulfluramid	Poison-bait form; low toxicity	Indoors: cockroaches; outdoors: ants
Tetrachlorvinphos	Dust or wettable-powder form; low toxicity	Outdoors: chiggers, ticks
Tetramethrin	Aerosol or dust form; low toxicity	Indoors: cockroaches, firebrats, silverfish; outdoors: biting flies

FUNGICIDES

TYPE	CHARACTERISTICS	USES
Copper sulfate	Aerosol form; toxic to fish and wildlife	Most plants
Benomyl	Aerosol or granular form; low toxicity	Most plants; less readily absorbed by woody types
Lime sulfur	Aerosol form; toxic to fish	Fruit, roses and trees as prevention in fall, winter or spring
Captan	Aerosol or dust form; toxic to fish	Most plants
Chlorothalonil	Aerosol form; toxic to fish	Most plants; can be applied up to 3 days before harvest
Dinocap	Aerosol or dust form; toxic to fish	Most plants
Folpet	Aerosol or dust form; toxic to fish	Most plants; sometimes used in combination with pesticide
Iprodione	Aerosol form; toxic to fish	Lawns
Maneb	Aerosol form; toxic to fish	Most plants; sometimes used in combination with pesticide
Streptomycin	Aerosol form; low toxicity	Most plants; antibiotic
Sulfur	Aerosol or dust form; low toxicity	Most plants; do not apply within 4 weeks of use of dormant oil
Triforine	Aerosol form; toxic to fish	Roses and other flowers in spring and fall at intervals of 7 to 10 days; sometimes used in combination with pesticide

HERBICIDES

TYPE	CHARACTERISTICS	USES
Ammonium sulfamate	Post-emergent (remedial); not selective (untargeted); systemic (attacks roots)	Spring or fall: kills trees; woody plants; vines
2,4-D	Post-emergent (remedial); selective (targeted); systemic (attacks roots)	Spring or fall to lawns (not St. Augustine, centipede or bentgrass), sometimes with dicamba or mecoprop: kills broad-leafed weeds
DCPA (trade name: Dacthal)	Pre-emergent (preventive); selective (targeted)	Early spring or late fall to lawns and gardens, sometimes with fertilizer: kills germinating grass-type weeds, some broad-leafed weeds
Dicamba	Post-emergent (remedial); selective (targeted); systemic (attacks roots)	Spring or fall to lawns, with 2,4-D and/or mecoprop (use alone requires permit): kills many broad-leafed weeds
Glyphosate	Post-emergent (remedial); not selective (untargeted); systemic (attacks roots)	Timing of application varies with intended target: kills woody plants; vines; grass-type and broad-leafed weeds
Mecoprop	Post-emergent (remedial); selective (targeted); systemic (attacks roots)	Spring or fall to lawns, with 2,4-D and/or dicamba (use alone requires permit): kills many broad-leafed weeds
Methanearsonates (MSMA, DSMA)	Post-emergent (remedial); selective (targeted); some systemic effect (attacks roots)	Spring or fall to lawns (not St. Augustine, centipede or carpet), sometimes with 2,4-D: kills grass-type weeds
Siduron	Pre-emergent (preventive); selective (targeted)	Early spring or late fall to lawns (not St. Augustine, centipede or zoysia), sometimes with fertilizer: kills germinating grass-type weeds
Triclopyr	Post-emergent (remedial); not selective (untargeted); systemic (attacks roots)	Spring or fall: kills trees; woody plants; vines

GRASSES

TYPE	CHARACTERISTICS	USES
Kentucky bluegrass	Cool-season grass; hardy and popular Shade of color differs with variety Forms dense turf Good drought tolerance; medium disease resistance	Planted by seeding: 2 to 4 pounds per 1000 square feet; sodding Maximum mowing height of 1 1/2 to 2 1/2 inches
Perennial ryegrass	Cool-season grass; grows rapidly Shade of color differs with variety Often mixed with other grass or used for overseeding Moderate drought tolerance; medium disease resistance	Planted by seeding: 6 to 10 pounds per 1000 square feet; sodding Maximum mowing height of 1 1/2 to 2 1/2 inches
Tall fescue	Cool-season grass; low maintenance (grows slowly) Medium to dark green color May form clumps if not heavily seeded Good drought tolerance; high disease resistance	Planted by seeding: 8 to 10 pounds per 1000 square feet; sodding Maximum mowing height of 2 to 3 inches
Fine fescue	Cool-season grass; good shade tolerance Medium green color Forms fine-textured, open turf Moderate drought tolerance; medium disease resistance	Planted by seeding: 2 to 4 pounds per 1000 square feet; sodding Maximum mowing height of 1 1/2 to 2 1/2 inches
Bahia grass	Warm-season grass; hardy (but poor salt tolerance) and low maintenance (grows slowly) Light green color Forms coarse-textured turf; prone to forming excessive thatch Excellent drought tolerance; medium disease resistance	Planted by seeding: 4 to 5 pounds per 1000 square feet; sodding; sprigging; plugging Maximum mowing height of 2 to 3 inches
Bermuda grass	Warm-season grass; hardy and grows quickly Dark green to bluish color Establishes quickly; prone to forming excessive thatch Excellent drought tolerance; medium disease resistance	Planted by seeding: 2 to 4 pounds per 1000 square feet; sodding; sprigging; plugging Maximum mowing height of 3/4 inch to 1 1/2 inches
St. Augustine grass	Warm-season grass; good shade and salt tolerance Dark green to bluish color Forms coarse-textured, dense turf; prone to forming excessive thatch Moderate drought tolerance; poor disease resistance	Planted by sodding; sprigging; plugging Maximum mowing height of 1 1/2 to 2 1/2 inches
Centipede grass	Warm-season grass; low maintenance (grows slowly) and winter dormancy begins early Shade of color differs with variety Establishes slowly; prone to forming excessive thatch Moderate drought tolerance; medium disease resistance	Planted by sodding; sprigging; plugging Maximum mowing height of 1 inch to 2 inches
Zoysia grass	Warm-season grass; hardy and low maintenance (grows slowly) with good shade and salt tolerance Shade of color differs with variety Establishes very slowly; prone to forming excessive thatch Good drought tolerance; medium disease resistance	Planted by sodding; sprigging; plugging Maximum mowing height of 1/2 to 1 inch

SOIL NUTRIENTS

TYPE	CHARACTERISTICS	TYPE	CHARACTERISTICS
NITROGEN (N)		**PHOSPHORUS (P) (continued)**	
Ammonium nitrate	Fast release; high burn potential	**Phosphate rock**	Released faster when finely ground Mineral source of phosphorus Best applied one or two months after amendment of animal manure
Ammonium sulfate	Fast release; high burn potential May harm beneficial soil bacteria; may acidify soil	**Superphosphate**	Medium release; low burn potential Treated with sulfuric acid
Blood meal	Organic, slow release; low burn potential Long-term source of phosphorus	**POTASSIUM (K)**	
Sodium nitrate	Fast release; low burn potential	**Potassium chloride (muriate of potash)**	Fast release; high burn potential May acidify soil
Urea	Organic, may be fast or slow release; low or medium burn potential	**Potassium nitrate**	Fast release; high burn potential Also contains nitrogen
PHOSPHORUS (P)		**Potassium sulfate**	Fast release; medium burn potential May acidify soil
Ammonium phosphate	Fast release; high burn potential Also contains nitrogen	**Granite dust**	Slow release; best applied with amendment (ashes, manure or compost)
Bone meal	Organic, slow release; low burn potential Recommended for bulb planting		

SOIL AMENDMENTS AND MULCHES

TYPE	CHARACTERISTICS	USES
Agricultural byproducts: buckwheat, cocoa bean, cottonseed or peanut hulls; corncobs or cornstalks	Cocoa bean hulls slightly acidic; corncobs or cornstalks nitrogen-poor	Amendment: corncobs or cornstalks grinded or chopped and added after nitrogen-rich material Mulch: applied 2 to 4 inches deep (corncobs 6 inches deep); cottonseed hulls covered with thin layer of another mulch to prevent blowing away
Aluminum foil or foil-backed paper	No nutritional value; may inhibit aphids and other insects Does not permit water penetration; may burn leaves	Mulch: staked down or covered with thin layer of another mulch to prevent blowing away
Compost	Excellent source of organic matter with variable composition depending on contents; decomposes quickly	Amendment: added only when well decomposed Mulch: applied 1 inch to 2 inches deep
Crushed rock; stone chips	No nutritional value Water penetrates easily	Mulch: applied 1 inch to 2 inches deep; over polyethelene sheets for best weed control
Farm animal manure: cattle; horse; poultry; sheep; swine	Excellent source of organic matter; poultry manure especially nitrogen-rich May be salty and have strong odor	Amendment: composted prior to adding Mulch: applied 1 inch to 2 inches deep
Hardwood ashes	Excellent source of potash; alkaline	Amendment: added to acidic soil Mulch: applied 1 inch to 2 inches deep
Hay; salt-marsh hay	Light and porous; alfalfa hay especially nitrogen-rich May contain weed seeds	Amendment: excellent for vegetable and flower gardens; salt-marsh hay good for new lawns Mulch: applied 6 to 8 inches deep (salt-marsh hay 4 to 6 inches deep); good as winter mulch when applied 8 to 12 inches deep
Lawn clippings	Organic matter and micronutrients must be added; decompose quickly Inhibit water penetration if packed down	Amendment: not added if recently treated with herbicide Mulch: applied 2 to 3 inches deep (less deep if green)
Leaves	Light and porous	Amendment: dried and shredded prior to adding Mulch: applied 3 to 4 inches deep; excellent as winter mulch when mixed with straw or hay and applied 8 to 12 inches deep
Paper (including newspaper, but not glossy or color pages)	Adds organic matter and trace nutrients; slightly alkaline May inhibit water penetration	Amendment: shredded or torn prior to adding to help water penetration and speed decomposition Mulch: applied flat in thicknesses of 5 to 6 pages; moistened or covered with thin layer of another mulch to prevent blowing away
Peat moss	Excellent source of organic matter; acidic and decomposes slowly Light and porous; may form crust on soil Not suitable for arid climates	Amendment: good for acid-loving plants and new lawns; helps to aerate clay soil or to improve water retention of sandy soil Mulch: applied 2 to 3 inches deep; excellent as winter mulch
Polyethylene sheets (clear or black)	No nutritional value; black inhibits weeds Do not permit water penetration	Mulch: staked down or covered with thin layer of another mulch to prevent blowing away
Sand	No nutritional value Improves water penetration of clay soil; must be medium- or coarse-grained	Amendment: best added in mix of 1 part sand to 1 part peat moss and 2 parts cultivated soil
Seaweed	Light and porous	Amendment: washed prior to adding if salty Mulch: applied 2 to 4 inches deep
Straw	Light and porous; nitrogen-poor	Amendment: added after nitrogen-rich material Mulch: applied 6 to 8 inches deep; good as winter mulch when applied 8 to 12 inches deep
Wood byproducts: ground bark; pine needles; sawdust	Organic matter and nutrients must be added; slightly acidic Ground bark and sawdust may inhibit water penetration if not cultivated periodically	Amendment: added after nitrogen-rich material Mulch: applied 2 to 4 inches deep

TOOLS AND SAFETY EQUIPMENT

ELECTRIC DRILL

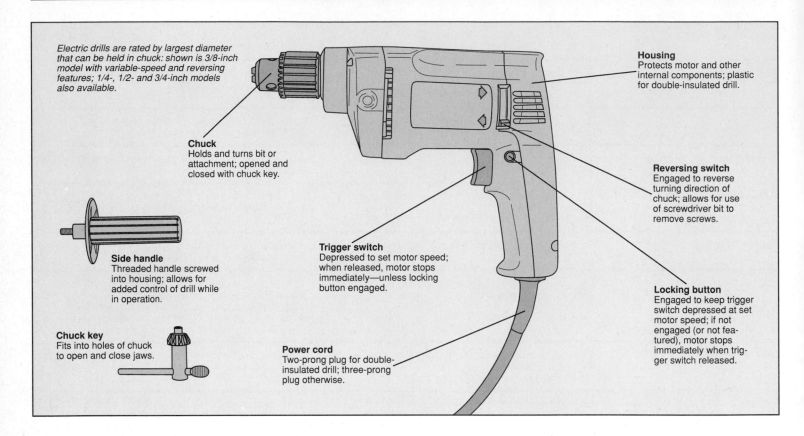

Electric drills are rated by largest diameter that can be held in chuck: shown is 3/8-inch model with variable-speed and reversing features; 1/4-, 1/2- and 3/4-inch models also available.

Chuck
Holds and turns bit or attachment; opened and closed with chuck key.

Side handle
Threaded handle screwed into housing; allows for added control of drill while in operation.

Chuck key
Fits into holes of chuck to open and close jaws.

Trigger switch
Depressed to set motor speed; when released, motor stops immediately—unless locking button engaged.

Power cord
Two-prong plug for double-insulated drill; three-prong plug otherwise.

Housing
Protects motor and other internal components; plastic for double-insulated drill.

Reversing switch
Engaged to reverse turning direction of chuck; allows for use of screwdriver bit to remove screws.

Locking button
Engaged to keep trigger switch depressed at set motor speed; if not engaged (or not featured), motor stops immediately when trigger switch released.

ELECTRIC DRILL BITS

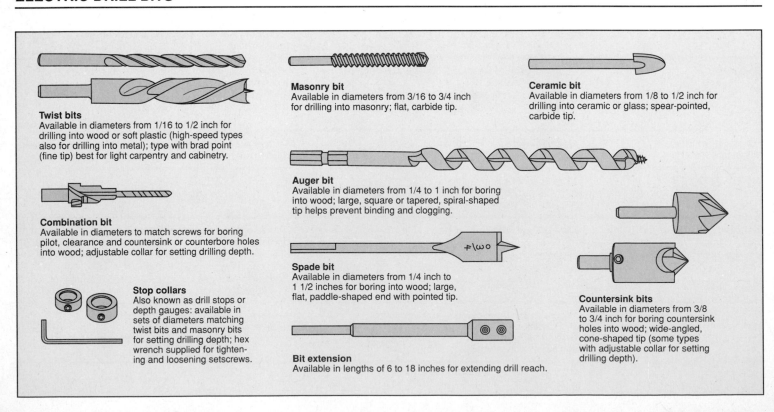

Twist bits
Available in diameters from 1/16 to 1/2 inch for drilling into wood or soft plastic (high-speed types also for drilling into metal); type with brad point (fine tip) best for light carpentry and cabinetry.

Combination bit
Available in diameters to match screws for boring pilot, clearance and countersink or counterbore holes into wood; adjustable collar for setting drilling depth.

Stop collars
Also known as drill stops or depth gauges: available in sets of diameters matching twist bits and masonry bits for setting drilling depth; hex wrench supplied for tightening and loosening setscrews.

Masonry bit
Available in diameters from 3/16 to 3/4 inch for drilling into masonry; flat, carbide tip.

Auger bit
Available in diameters from 1/4 to 1 inch for boring into wood; large, square or tapered, spiral-shaped tip helps prevent binding and clogging.

Spade bit
Available in diameters from 1/4 inch to 1 1/2 inches for boring into wood; large, flat, paddle-shaped end with pointed tip.

Bit extension
Available in lengths of 6 to 18 inches for extending drill reach.

Ceramic bit
Available in diameters from 1/8 to 1/2 inch for drilling into ceramic or glass; spear-pointed, carbide tip.

Countersink bits
Available in diameters from 3/8 to 3/4 inch for boring countersink holes into wood; wide-angled, cone-shaped tip (some types with adjustable collar for setting drilling depth).

ELECTRIC DRILL ACCESSORIES

Arbor
Spindle with two balanced flange washers held by bolt; adapts drill for use with attachment such as buffing wheel, grinding wheel or wire brush.

Grinding wheel
Available in diameters from 1 inch to 3 inches in coarse, medium and fine grades; used with arbor to adapt drill for sharpening cutting edges of metal: blades of tools such as chisels, knives, planes and scissors.

Mounted grinding points
Available in kits in variety of diameters and shapes; adapts drill for grinding metal or plastic: enlarging holes; deburring edges.

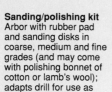

Sanding/polishing kit
Arbor with rubber pad and sanding disks in coarse, medium and fine grades (and may come with polishing bonnet of cotton or lamb's wool); adapts drill for use as sander or polisher.

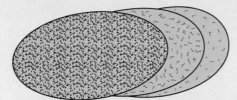

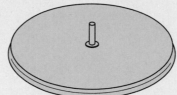

Wire brushes
Available in coarse or fine grades as wheel (diameters from 2 to 4 inches) or mounted cup (diameters from 2 to 3 inches) to adapt drill for use in polishing metal or removing paint and rust: wheel type used with arbor; mounted cup type used for corners and other places hard to reach.

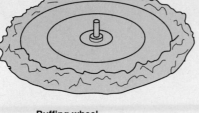

Buffing wheel
Arbor with rubber pad and polishing bonnet of cotton or lamb's wool; adapts drill for use as polisher.

Hole saws
Available in kits in variety of diameters; used with arbor and high-speed bit as pilot to adapt drill for cutting holes through wood, soft plastic or metal: standard-cutting type for depth of up to 1 1/4 inches; deep-cutting type for depth of up to 1 3/4 inches.

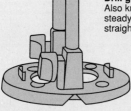

Drill guide
Also known as boring jig; used for steadying drill to ensure boring of straight and perpendicular hole.

Paint mixer
Available in blade diameters from 1 1/2 to 4 inches and shaft lengths from 16 to 20 inches; adapts drill to stir paint or other liquid.

Lawn mower blade sharpener
Grinding wheel of special design; used with arbor to adapt drill for sharpening cutting edges of metal: rotary blades of tools such as lawn mowers and garden tillers.

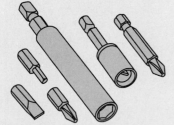

Screwdriver bits
Available in sets to fit heads of slotted, Phillips or Robertson screws of various diameters; adapt drill for use as screwdriver.

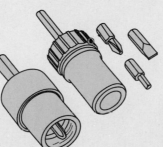

Clutch drivers
Available in variety of models to adapt drill for use in installing screws: fixed-bit type that drives to preset depth; interchangeable-bit type that drives to adjustable depth.

CIRCULAR SAW

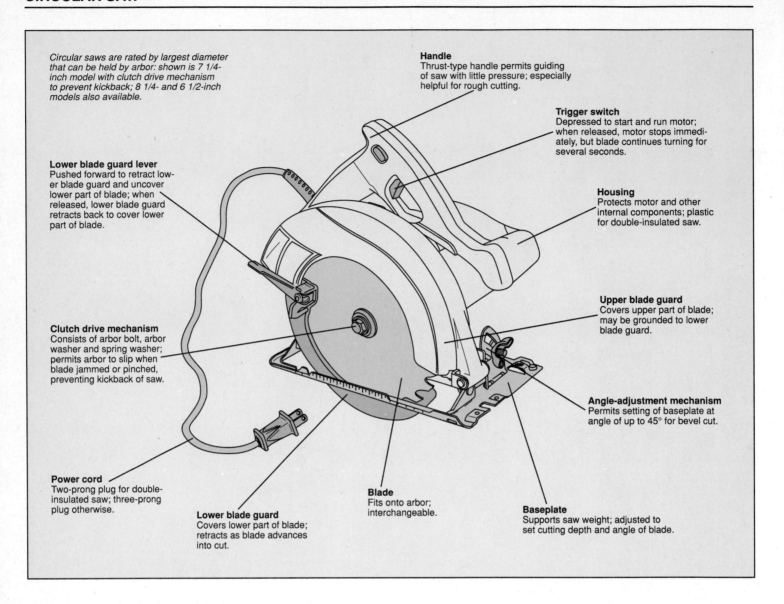

Circular saws are rated by largest diameter that can be held by arbor: shown is 7 1/4-inch model with clutch drive mechanism to prevent kickback; 8 1/4- and 6 1/2-inch models also available.

Handle
Thrust-type handle permits guiding of saw with little pressure; especially helpful for rough cutting.

Trigger switch
Depressed to start and run motor; when released, motor stops immediately, but blade continues turning for several seconds.

Lower blade guard lever
Pushed forward to retract lower blade guard and uncover lower part of blade; when released, lower blade guard retracts back to cover lower part of blade.

Housing
Protects motor and other internal components; plastic for double-insulated saw.

Upper blade guard
Covers upper part of blade; may be grounded to lower blade guard.

Clutch drive mechanism
Consists of arbor bolt, arbor washer and spring washer; permits arbor to slip when blade jammed or pinched, preventing kickback of saw.

Angle-adjustment mechanism
Permits setting of baseplate at angle of up to 45° for bevel cut.

Power cord
Two-prong plug for double-insulated saw; three-prong plug otherwise.

Lower blade guard
Covers lower part of blade; retracts as blade advances into cut.

Blade
Fits onto arbor; interchangeable.

Baseplate
Supports saw weight; adjusted to set cutting depth and angle of blade.

CIRCULAR SAW ACCESSORIES

Miter guide
Held or clamped in position on workpiece and adjusted to cutting angle from 0° to 90°; helps to ensure precise cutting of miter.

Rip guide
Connected to baseplate and adjusted for rip cut (along wood grain) parallel to edge of board; ensures precise cutting to width of up to 6 inches.

Water feed attachment
Spray fork mounted on baseplate and connected by hose to faucet; helps prevent overheating of masonry abrasive blade.

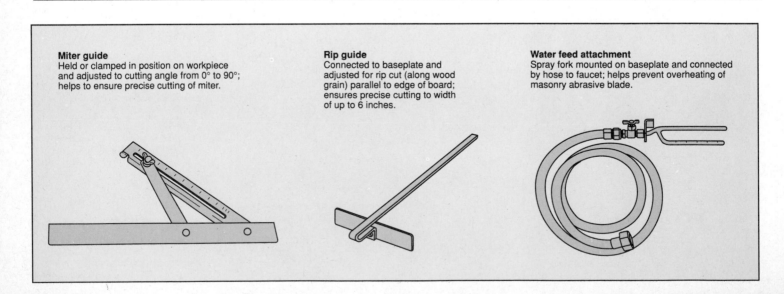

CIRCULAR SAW BLADES

TYPE	CHARACTERISTICS	USES
Standard combination blade	All-purpose blade of high-speed steel; may be carbide-tipped Blade design includes crosscutting teeth (beveled, pointed shape) and rip-cutting teeth (flat, chiseled shape)	General rough carpentry: slow, rough cuts of softwood, hardwood, plywood or board product; crosscuts (across wood grain), rip cuts (along wood grain) and miter cuts
Master combination (planer) blade	All-purpose blade of high-speed steel; may be carbide-tipped Blade design includes crosscutting teeth (beveled, pointed shape) and rip-cutting teeth (flat, chiseled shape)	General fine carpentry and cabinetry: fast, fine cuts of softwood, hardwood, plywood or board product; smooth crosscuts (across wood grain), rip cuts (along wood grain) and miter cuts
Carbide-tipped blade	All-purpose blade with teeth of tungsten-carbide; more expensive and stays sharper longer than conventional high-speed steel Range of blade designs: combination teeth (crosscutting and rip-cutting shape); crosscutting teeth (beveled, pointed shape); rip-cutting teeth (flat, chiseled shape); plywood-cutting teeth (fine set, fine-pointed shape)	General fine carpentry and cabinetry: fast, fine cuts of softwood, hardwood, plywood or board product (also plastic laminate); very smooth crosscuts (across wood grain), rip cuts (along wood grain) and miter cuts
Plywood (paneling) blade	Specialty blade of high-speed steel; may be carbide-tipped Blade design of fine teeth with no set (hollow ground; unbeveled) or little set (slight bevel) prevents splintering, providing smooth cut edge needing little finishing	Fine carpentry and cabinetry: fine, finished cuts of plywood, board product or veneer (also thin plastic)
Crosscut (cutoff) blade	Specialty blade of high-speed steel; may be carbide-tipped Blade design of evenly-spaced, beveled, pointed-shape teeth provides smooth crosscut edge needing little finishing; larger teeth required for softwood than for hardwood to carry off sawdust	Fine carpentry and cabinetry: fine, finished crosscuts (across wood grain)
Rip blade	Specialty blade of high-speed steel; may be carbide-tipped Blade design of evenly-spaced, flat, chiseled-shape teeth provides rip-cutting efficiency, preventing clogging and overheating	Rip cuts (along wood grain) of softwood or hardwood; not suited for plywood or board product
Masonry abrasive blade	Specialty abrasive blade; smooth-edged wheel without teeth: typically of silicon-carbide and usually about 1/8 inch thick Range of types for different hardnesses; may require use with water feed attachment to prevent overheating	Cutting of masonry: brick (including common, fire and refractory), stone, concrete; also ceramic tile
Metal abrasive blade	Specialty abrasive blade; smooth-edged wheel without teeth: typically of aluminum-oxide and usually about 1/8 inch thick Range of types for different hardnesses	Cutting of metal: aluminum, brass, bronze, copper, steel

SABER SAW

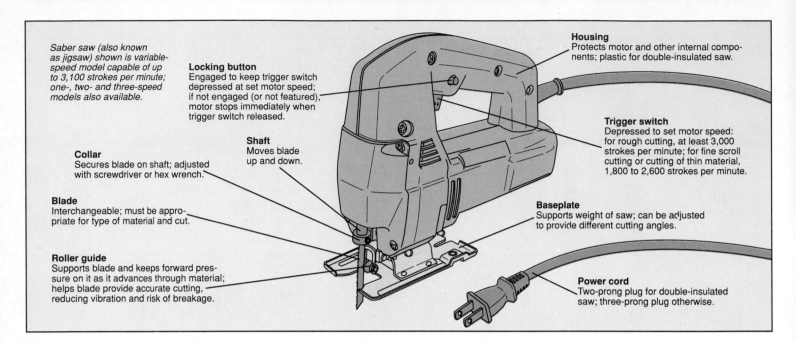

Saber saw (also known as jigsaw) shown is variable-speed model capable of up to 3,100 strokes per minute; one-, two- and three-speed models also available.

Locking button
Engaged to keep trigger switch depressed at set motor speed; if not engaged (or not featured), motor stops immediately when trigger switch released.

Housing
Protects motor and other internal components; plastic for double-insulated saw.

Shaft
Moves blade up and down.

Trigger switch
Depressed to set motor speed: for rough cutting, at least 3,000 strokes per minute; for fine scroll cutting or cutting of thin material, 1,800 to 2,600 strokes per minute.

Collar
Secures blade on shaft; adjusted with screwdriver or hex wrench.

Blade
Interchangeable; must be appropriate for type of material and cut.

Baseplate
Supports weight of saw; can be adjusted to provide different cutting angles.

Roller guide
Supports blade and keeps forward pressure on it as it advances through material; helps blade provide accurate cutting, reducing vibration and risk of breakage.

Power cord
Two-prong plug for double-insulated saw; three-prong plug otherwise.

SABER SAW BLADES

TYPE	CHARACTERISTICS	USES
Standard cutting	Length of 3 to 4 1/4 inches with 6 to 10 teeth per inch	For high-speed standard cuts of wood: low-range teeth per inch for rough cuts; mid-range teeth per inch for medium cuts; high-range teeth per inch for fine cuts
Flush cutting	Length of 3 inches with 7 teeth per inch Design allows cutting to end flush at inside edge	For high-speed cuts of wood more than 1/4 inch thick
Double cutting	Length of 3 inches with 7 or 10 teeth per inch Design allows forward and backward cutting at equal speed	For cuts of wood: 7 teeth per inch for high-speed rough cuts; 10 teeth per inch for moderate-speed medium cuts
Scroll cutting	Length of 2 1/2 inches with 10 teeth per inch Design allows for tiny, intricate cutting	For moderate-speed smooth cuts of wood or plastic 1/4 to 1 inch thick; curves with radius as small as 1/8 inch
Fleam-ground cutting	Length of 4 inches with 10 teeth per inch Design allows shredding-type cutting	For moderate-speed smooth cuts of hard, green or wet wood 1/4 inch to 1 1/2 inches thick
Metal cutting	Length of 2 3/4 to 3 inches with 13 to 32 teeth per inch	For high-speed standard cuts of steel 1/16 to 3/8 inch thick; aluminum or copper 1/8 to 1/4 inch thick; plastic 1/4 to 1/2 inch thick: range of teeth per inch that lets at least two teeth contact material
Knife cutting	Length of 3 inches with knife-cutting edge	For high-speed smooth cuts of cardboard, composition tile, leather or rubber
Plaster cutting	Length of 3 5/8 inches with 9 teeth per inch Design of V-shaped teeth allows constant abrading action	For high-speed rough cuts of drywall, plaster, masonry or high-density plastic
Skip-tooth cutting	Length of 3 inches with 5 teeth per inch Design of extra-large gullets helps prevent clogging	For high-speed rough cuts of plastic or wood

BELT SANDER

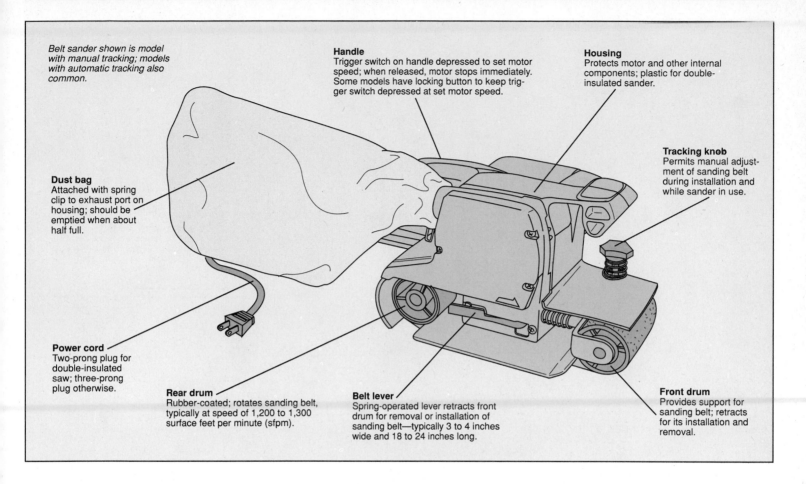

Belt sander shown is model with manual tracking; models with automatic tracking also common.

Handle
Trigger switch on handle depressed to set motor speed; when released, motor stops immediately. Some models have locking button to keep trigger switch depressed at set motor speed.

Housing
Protects motor and other internal components; plastic for double-insulated sander.

Tracking knob
Permits manual adjustment of sanding belt during installation and while sander in use.

Dust bag
Attached with spring clip to exhaust port on housing; should be emptied when about half full.

Power cord
Two-prong plug for double-insulated saw; three-prong plug otherwise.

Rear drum
Rubber-coated; rotates sanding belt, typically at speed of 1,200 to 1,300 surface feet per minute (sfpm).

Belt lever
Spring-operated lever retracts front drum for removal or installation of sanding belt—typically 3 to 4 inches wide and 18 to 24 inches long.

Front drum
Provides support for sanding belt; retracts for its installation and removal.

ORBITAL SANDER

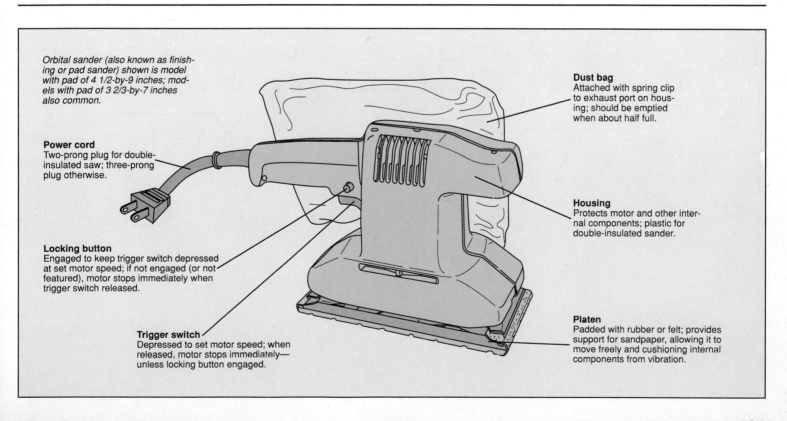

Orbital sander (also known as finishing or pad sander) shown is model with pad of 4 1/2-by-9 inches; models with pad of 3 2/3-by-7 inches also common.

Dust bag
Attached with spring clip to exhaust port on housing; should be emptied when about half full.

Power cord
Two-prong plug for double-insulated saw; three-prong plug otherwise.

Housing
Protects motor and other internal components; plastic for double-insulated sander.

Locking button
Engaged to keep trigger switch depressed at set motor speed; if not engaged (or not featured), motor stops immediately when trigger switch released.

Trigger switch
Depressed to set motor speed; when released, motor stops immediately—unless locking button engaged.

Platen
Padded with rubber or felt; provides support for sandpaper, allowing it to move freely and cushioning internal components from vibration.

ROUTER

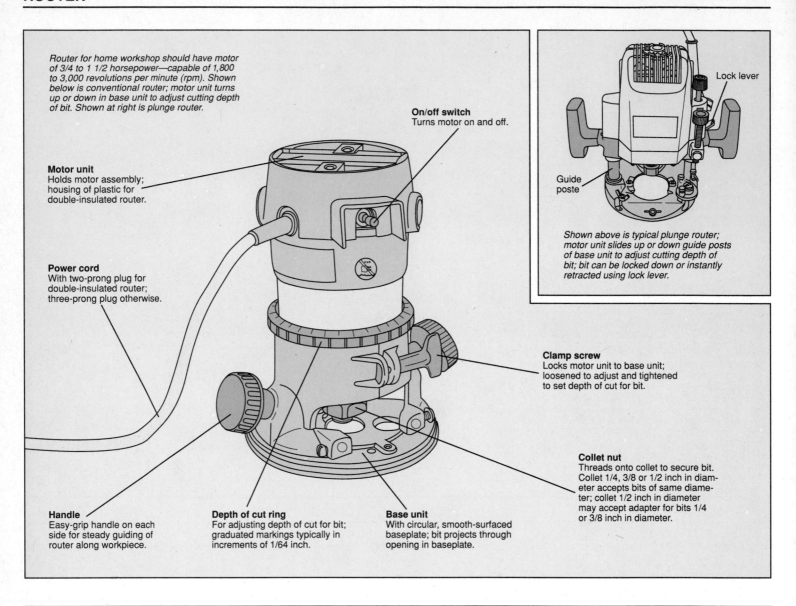

Router for home workshop should have motor of 3/4 to 1 1/2 horsepower—capable of 1,800 to 3,000 revolutions per minute (rpm). Shown below is conventional router; motor unit turns up or down in base unit to adjust cutting depth of bit. Shown at right is plunge router.

Lock lever

Guide poste

Shown above is typical plunge router; motor unit slides up or down guide posts of base unit to adjust cutting depth of bit; bit can be locked down or instantly retracted using lock lever.

On/off switch
Turns motor on and off.

Motor unit
Holds motor assembly; housing of plastic for double-insulated router.

Power cord
With two-prong plug for double-insulated router; three-prong plug otherwise.

Clamp screw
Locks motor unit to base unit; loosened to adjust and tightened to set depth of cut for bit.

Collet nut
Threads onto collet to secure bit. Collet 1/4, 3/8 or 1/2 inch in diameter accepts bits of same diameter; collet 1/2 inch in diameter may accept adapter for bits 1/4 or 3/8 inch in diameter.

Handle
Easy-grip handle on each side for steady guiding of router along workpiece.

Depth of cut ring
For adjusting depth of cut for bit; graduated markings typically in increments of 1/64 inch.

Base unit
With circular, smooth-surfaced baseplate; bit projects through opening in baseplate.

ROUTER ACCESSORIES

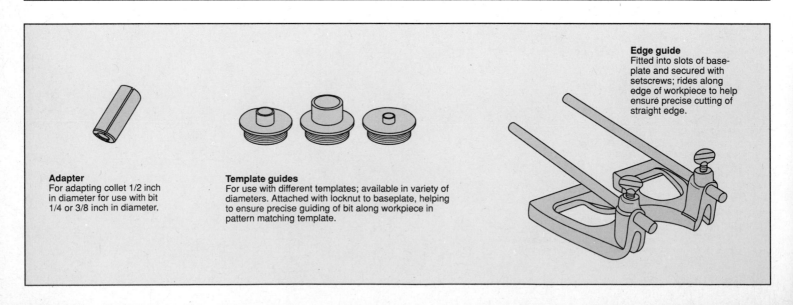

Adapter
For adapting collet 1/2 inch in diameter for use with bit 1/4 or 3/8 inch in diameter.

Template guides
For use with different templates; available in variety of diameters. Attached with locknut to baseplate, helping to ensure precise guiding of bit along workpiece in pattern matching template.

Edge guide
Fitted into slots of baseplate and secured with setscrews; rides along edge of workpiece to help ensure precise cutting of straight edge.

ROUTER BITS

GROOVE CUTTERS

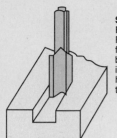

Straight bit
Flat bottom with straight sides. For general stock removal: flat-bottomed grooves; rabbets; dadoes; mortises; carvings. Typically available in high-speed steel, carbide-tipped or solid carbide.

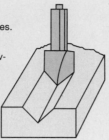

V-groove bit
Pointed tip and beveled, 45°-angle sides. For ornamental stock removal: V-shaped grooves; carvings; lettering; chamfers. Typically available in high-speed steel, carbide-tipped or solid carbide.

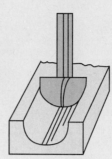

Mortising bit
Hollowed bottom with straight sides. For quick, clean, heavy stock removal: mortises; rabbets; dadoes. Typically available in high-speed steel, carbide-tipped or solid carbide.

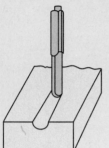

Veining bit
Round bottom with straight sides. For ornamental stock removal: grooves; freehand carvings; small coves; inlays; lettering. Typically available in high-speed steel, carbide-tipped or solid carbide.

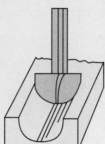

Core-box bit
Round bottom and sides. For ornamental stock removal: round-bottomed grooves; carvings; contours. Typically available in high-speed steel, carbide-tipped or solid carbide.

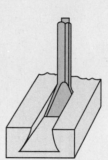

Dovetail bit
Flat bottom with flared sides. For quick, clean stock removal: dovetail joints; dadoes. Typically available in high-speed steel, carbide-tipped or solid carbide.

EDGE CUTTERS

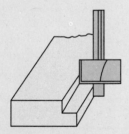

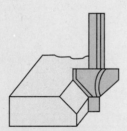

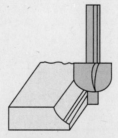

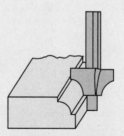

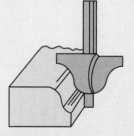

Rabbet bit
Piloted bit with flat bottom and straight sides. For cutting rabbeted or stepped edge. Typically available in high-speed steel, carbide-tipped or solid carbide.

Chamfering bit
Piloted bit with beveled, 45°-angle sides. For cutting decorative edge. Typically available in high-speed steel, carbide-tipped or solid carbide.

Cove bit
Piloted bit similar in shape to core-box bit. For cutting decorative edge; concave edge of joint for dropleaf table. Typically available in high-speed steel, carbide-tipped or solid carbide.

Beading bit
Piloted bit with flat bottom and concave sides. For cutting decorative edge; convex edge of joint for dropleaf table. Typically available in high-speed steel, carbide-tipped or solid carbide.

Roman ogee bit
Piloted bit with round bottom and concave sides; without pilot known as ogee bit. For cutting decorative edge. Typically available in high-speed steel, carbide-tipped or solid carbide.

SPECIALTY CUTTERS

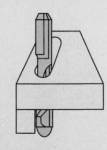

Panel pilot bit
Straight sides with pointed tip for drilling. For making cutouts; cutting lattice work; edge trimming of veneer. Typically available in high-speed steel, carbide-tipped or solid carbide.

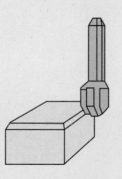

Laminate trimming bit
Range of styles and shapes; type shown with straight sides and beveled tip. For edge trimming of laminate or veneer. Typically available in high-speed steel, carbide-tipped or solid carbide.

HAMMERS AND MALLETS

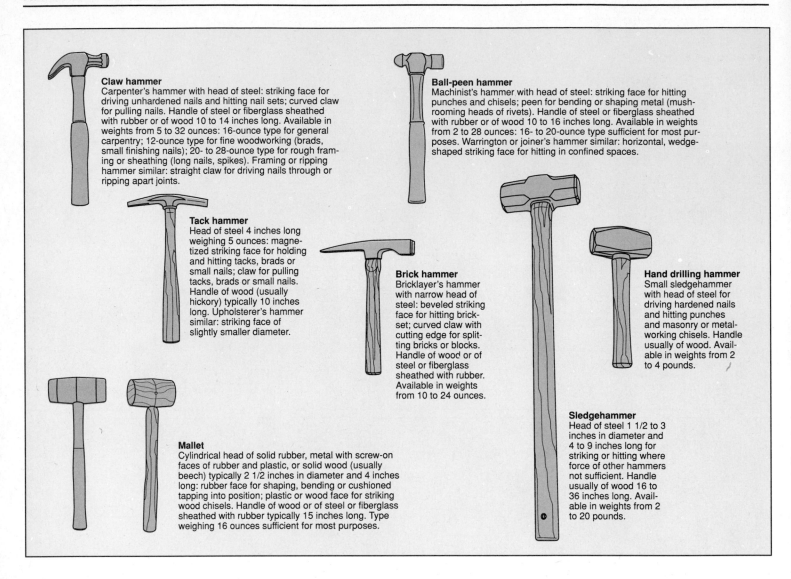

Claw hammer
Carpenter's hammer with head of steel: striking face for driving unhardened nails and hitting nail sets; curved claw for pulling nails. Handle of steel or fiberglass sheathed with rubber or of wood 10 to 14 inches long. Available in weights from 5 to 32 ounces: 16-ounce type for general carpentry; 12-ounce type for fine woodworking (brads, small finishing nails); 20- to 28-ounce type for rough framing or sheathing (long nails, spikes). Framing or ripping hammer similar: straight claw for driving nails through or ripping apart joints.

Ball-peen hammer
Machinist's hammer with head of steel: striking face for hitting punches and chisels; peen for bending or shaping metal (mushrooming heads of rivets). Handle of steel or fiberglass sheathed with rubber or of wood 10 to 16 inches long. Available in weights from 2 to 28 ounces: 16- to 20-ounce type sufficient for most purposes. Warrington or joiner's hammer similar: horizontal, wedge-shaped striking face for hitting in confined spaces.

Tack hammer
Head of steel 4 inches long weighing 5 ounces: magnetized striking face for holding and hitting tacks, brads or small nails; claw for pulling tacks, brads or small nails. Handle of wood (usually hickory) typically 10 inches long. Upholsterer's hammer similar: striking face of slightly smaller diameter.

Brick hammer
Bricklayer's hammer with narrow head of steel: beveled striking face for hitting brickset; curved claw with cutting edge for splitting bricks or blocks. Handle of wood or of steel or fiberglass sheathed with rubber. Available in weights from 10 to 24 ounces.

Hand drilling hammer
Small sledgehammer with head of steel for driving hardened nails and hitting punches and masonry or metalworking chisels. Handle usually of wood. Available in weights from 2 to 4 pounds.

Mallet
Cylindrical head of solid rubber, metal with screw-on faces of rubber and plastic, or solid wood (usually beech) typically 2 1/2 inches in diameter and 4 inches long: rubber face for shaping, bending or cushioned tapping into position; plastic or wood face for striking wood chisels. Handle of wood or of steel or fiberglass sheathed with rubber typically 15 inches long. Type weighing 16 ounces sufficient for most purposes.

Sledgehammer
Head of steel 1 1/2 to 3 inches in diameter and 4 to 9 inches long for striking or hitting where force of other hammers not sufficient. Handle usually of wood 16 to 36 inches long. Available in weights from 2 to 20 pounds.

NAIL SETS AND PUNCHES

Nail set
For setting heads of finishing nails below surface; tips from 1/32 to 5/32 inch in diameter. Used with claw hammer.

Prick punch
Also known as dot punch. For marking hole locations and making starting holes for fasteners in metal, often prior to enlarging with center punch. Used with ball-peen hammer.

Starter punch
Also known as drift punch or solid punch. For use prior to pin punch in driving out bushings or fasteners such as cotter, shear or other pins from metal; lengths from 4 1/2 to 7 1/4 inches tapering to tip from 3/32 to 1/2 inch in diameter. Used with ball-peen hammer or hand drilling hammer.

Awl
Also known as scratch awl or bradawl. For scoring, marking hole locations and making starting holes for fasteners in wood, plastic or leather; steel blade 5 inches long with round, square or diamond-shaped tip. Used with hand pressure.

Center punch
Also known as nail punch. For marking hole locations and making starting holes for fasteners in metal or driving out shanks of pop rivets (heads removed); lengths from 3 1/2 to 7 inches tapering to tip 1/8 inch in diameter. Used with ball-peen hammer or hand drilling hammer.

Pin punch
For use following starter punch in driving out bushings or fasteners such as cotter, shear or other pins from metal; lengths from 4 1/2 to 6 1/4 inches tapering to tip from 3/32 to 3/8 inch in diameter. Used with ball-peen hammer or hand drilling hammer.

CHISELS

WOODWORKING CHISELS

Paring chisel
Thin blade with beveled sides; widths from 3/16 inch to 1 1/2 inches. For light, fine cutting of wood; used with hand pressure.

Mortise chisel
Narrow, thick, tapered, square-edged blade; widths of 1/4, 5/16, 3/8 and 1/2 inch most commonly used. For cutting mortises in wood; used with wooden mallet (if handle of wood) or ball-peen hammer (if handle metal-capped).

Firmer chisel
Also known as wood chisel. Thicker blade than paring chisel with square-edged (not beveled) sides; widths from 1/8 inch to 2 inches. For general, light or heavy, rough cutting of wood; used with hand pressure or wooden mallet (if handle of wood) or ball-peen hammer (if handle metal-capped).

Butt chisel
Short, thick blade with square-edged (not beveled) sides; widths from 1/4 inch to 2 inches. For heavy, rough cutting of wood; used with wooden mallet (if handle of wood) or ball-peen hammer (if handle metal-capped).

MASONRY CHISELS

Bull-point chisel
Also known as point or concrete chisel. Hexagonal-shaped shaft from 12 to 18 inches long with tapered tip. For breaking bricks, stone, concrete, mortar or stucco; used with ball-peen hammer or hand drilling hammer.

Star drill
Hexagonal-shaped shaft 10 inches long with double-beveled, star-shaped tip. For making round holes in bricks, stone, concrete or stucco; used with hand drilling hammer.

Brickset
Also known as bricklayer's chisel, brick chisel, or mason's chisel. Blade with integral handle 7 inches long; widths of 3, 4 or 5 inches. For scoring and cutting bricks; used with hand drilling hammer.

Plugging chisel
Also known as seam drill. Fluted shaft 10 inches long with rectangular-shaped tip of 1/4 inch. For breaking mortar of joints between bricks, blocks or stone; used with ball-peen hammer or hand drilling hammer.

METALWORKING CHISELS

Cold chisel
Also known as flat chisel. Hexagonal-shaped shaft from 5 to 12 inches long with flat, tapered, straight tip of 3/16 to 1 inch. Used with ball-peen hammer or hand drilling hammer for general cutting of metal and shearing of fasteners in restricted space (hacksaw or tin snips cannot be used) or breaking drywall, plaster or masonry.

Round chisel
Also known as half-round chisel. Hexagonal-shaped shaft from 6 3/4 to 8 1/4 inches long with rounded, tapered, arrowhead-shaped tip. Used with ball-peen hammer or hand drilling hammer for cutting round-edged corners, grooves and channels in metal; fine adjustment (relocating or enlarging) of holes.

Cape chisel
Also known as crosscut chisel. Hexagonal-shaped shaft from 6 3/4 to 8 1/4 inches long with flat, tapered, arrowhead-shaped tip. Used with ball-peen hammer or hand drilling hammer for cutting square-edged corners, grooves and channels in metal.

Diamond-point chisel
Hexagonal-shaped shaft from 6 3/4 to 8 1/4 inches long with flat, tapered, square-shaped tip. Used with ball-peen hammer or hand drilling hammer for cutting or cleaning square-edged corners and V-shaped grooves in metal.

HANDSAWS

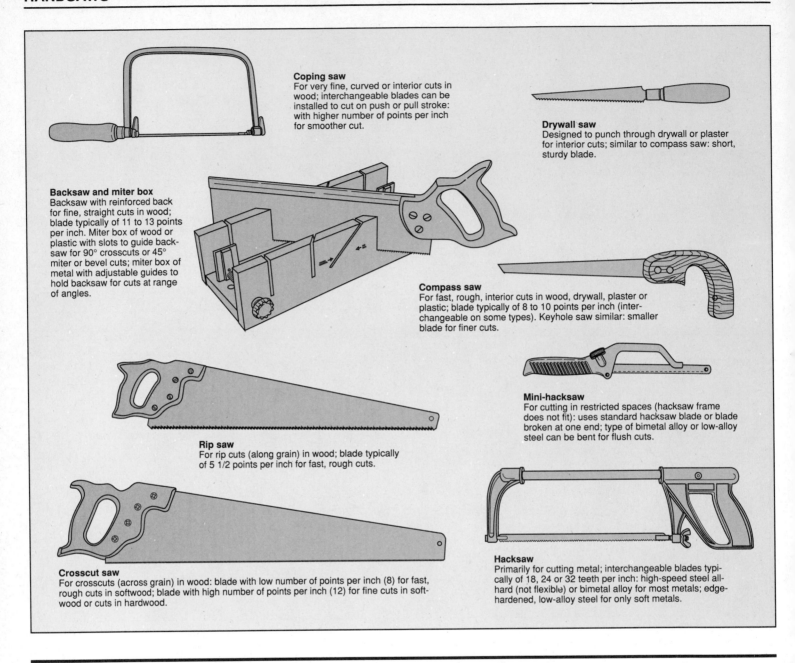

Coping saw
For very fine, curved or interior cuts in wood; interchangeable blades can be installed to cut on push or pull stroke: with higher number of points per inch for smoother cut.

Drywall saw
Designed to punch through drywall or plaster for interior cuts; similar to compass saw: short, sturdy blade.

Backsaw and miter box
Backsaw with reinforced back for fine, straight cuts in wood; blade typically of 11 to 13 points per inch. Miter box of wood or plastic with slots to guide backsaw for 90° crosscuts or 45° miter or bevel cuts; miter box of metal with adjustable guides to hold backsaw for cuts at range of angles.

Compass saw
For fast, rough, interior cuts in wood, drywall, plaster or plastic; blade typically of 8 to 10 points per inch (interchangeable on some types). Keyhole saw similar: smaller blade for finer cuts.

Mini-hacksaw
For cutting in restricted spaces (hacksaw frame does not fit): uses standard hacksaw blade or blade broken at one end; type of bimetal alloy or low-alloy steel can be bent for flush cuts.

Rip saw
For rip cuts (along grain) in wood; blade typically of 5 1/2 points per inch for fast, rough cuts.

Hacksaw
Primarily for cutting metal; interchangeable blades typically of 18, 24 or 32 teeth per inch: high-speed steel all-hard (not flexible) or bimetal alloy for most metals; edge-hardened, low-alloy steel for only soft metals.

Crosscut saw
For crosscuts (across grain) in wood: blade with low number of points per inch (8) for fast, rough cuts in softwood; blade with high number of points per inch (12) for fine cuts in softwood or cuts in hardwood.

PLANES

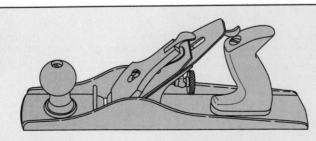 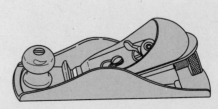

Bench plane
For trimming long edges of wood along grain: smoothing plane of 9 to 10 inches for fine, light cutting; jack plane of about 14 inches for rough cutting; jointer of about 22 inches for heavy cutting.

Block plane
For trimming end grain and edges of wood too short for bench plane; of different cutting widths: narrower for finer, lighter cutting; wider for rougher, heavier cutting.

FILES AND RASPS

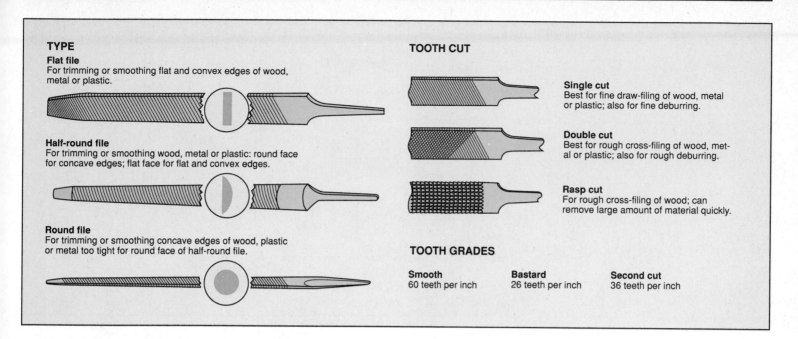

TYPE

Flat file
For trimming or smoothing flat and convex edges of wood, metal or plastic.

Half-round file
For trimming or smoothing wood, metal or plastic: round face for concave edges; flat face for flat and convex edges.

Round file
For trimming or smoothing concave edges of wood, plastic or metal too tight for round face of half-round file.

TOOTH CUT

Single cut
Best for fine draw-filing of wood, metal or plastic; also for fine deburring.

Double cut
Best for rough cross-filing of wood, metal or plastic; also for rough deburring.

Rasp cut
For rough cross-filing of wood; can remove large amount of material quickly.

TOOTH GRADES

Smooth
60 teeth per inch

Bastard
26 teeth per inch

Second cut
36 teeth per inch

KNIVES AND CUTTERS

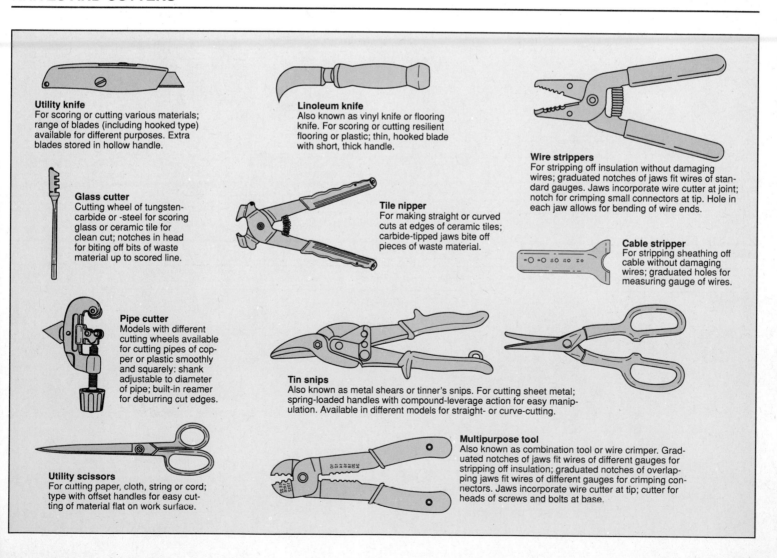

Utility knife
For scoring or cutting various materials; range of blades (including hooked type) available for different purposes. Extra blades stored in hollow handle.

Glass cutter
Cutting wheel of tungsten-carbide or -steel for scoring glass or ceramic tile for clean cut; notches in head for biting off bits of waste material up to scored line.

Pipe cutter
Models with different cutting wheels available for cutting pipes of copper or plastic smoothly and squarely: shank adjustable to diameter of pipe; built-in reamer for deburring cut edges.

Utility scissors
For cutting paper, cloth, string or cord; type with offset handles for easy cutting of material flat on work surface.

Linoleum knife
Also known as vinyl knife or flooring knife. For scoring or cutting resilient flooring or plastic; thin, hooked blade with short, thick handle.

Tile nipper
For making straight or curved cuts at edges of ceramic tiles; carbide-tipped jaws bite off pieces of waste material.

Tin snips
Also known as metal shears or tinner's snips. For cutting sheet metal; spring-loaded handles with compound-leverage action for easy manipulation. Available in different models for straight- or curve-cutting.

Multipurpose tool
Also known as combination tool or wire crimper. Graduated notches of jaws fit wires of different gauges for stripping off insulation; graduated notches of overlapping jaws fit wires of different gauges for crimping connectors. Jaws incorporate wire cutter at tip; cutter for heads of screws and bolts at base.

Wire strippers
For stripping off insulation without damaging wires; graduated notches of jaws fit wires of standard gauges. Jaws incorporate wire cutter at joint; notch for crimping small connectors at tip. Hole in each jaw allows for bending of wire ends.

Cable stripper
For stripping sheathing off cable without damaging wires; graduated holes for measuring gauge of wires.

SCREWDRIVERS

   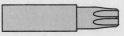

Flat tip
Also known as standard, straight-slot or mechanic's screwdriver. Fits head of slotted screws: 1/4 inch for No. 6 to No. 8 screws; 5/16 inch for No. 8 to No. 12 screws; 3/8 inch for No. 12 to No. 16 screws; 7/16 inch for No. 16 to No. 20 screws; 1/2 inch for No. 20 to No. 24 screws. Shank length of 6 to 8 inches common.

Phillips tip
Also known as cross-head or star screwdriver. Fits head of Phillips screws: No. 0 for No. 0 and No. 1 screws; No. 1 for No. 2 to No. 4 screws; No. 2 for No. 5 to No. 9 screws; No. 3 for No. 10 to No. 16 screws; No. 4 for No. 18 to No. 24 screws. Shank length of 6 to 8 inches common.

Torx tip
Fits head of torx screws: usually available in sizes of T-10, T-15, T-20, T-25 and T-30 for torx 10 to torx 30 screws. Shank length of 6 to 8 inches common.

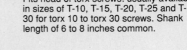

Cabinet tip
Fits head of slotted screws (for work in recesses or narrow openings): 3/16 inch for No. 6 to No. 8 screws. Shank length of 3 to 10 inches common.

Robertson tip
Also known as square-head screwdriver. Fits head of Robertson screws: No. 0 for No. 3 and No. 4 screws; No. 1 for No. 5 to No. 7 screws; No. 2 for No. 8 to No. 10 screws; No. 3 for No. 12 to No. 14 screws; No. 4 for No. 16 to No. 24 screws. Shank length of 6 to 8 inches common.

SPECIALTY SCREWDRIVERS

  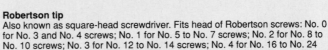

Ratchet screwdriver
Handle with ratchet mechanism permits constant grip for fast turning of screws; typically available with interchangeable flat, Phillips and Robertson tips of various sizes.

Jeweler's screwdrivers
For turning of tiny screws, especially in restricted places; typically available in sets: handle with interchangeable flat (0.025 to 3/32 inch), Phillips (No. 0) and awl-shaped tips.

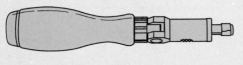 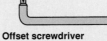

Nut drivers
For turning of hex-headed screws or bolts and hex nuts; typically available in socket sizes of 3/32 to 3/8 inch with shank length of 3 inches.

Stubby screwdriver
For leveraged turning of screws in restricted spaces; typically available in 1/4-inch flat tip and No. 2 Phillips tip with shank length of 1 1/2 inches.

Offset screwdriver
Also known as cranked screwdriver. For turning of screws in restricted spaces; typically available in double 1/4-inch flat tips and No. 2 Phillips tips with shank length of 3 inches.

WRENCHES

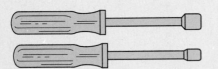

Adjustable wrench
For holding and light turning of hex or square nuts and bolt or screw heads through range of sizes. Typically available in lengths of 4 to 36 inches; common 10-inch type can grip diameter of up to 1 1/4 inches.

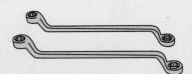

Box wrenches
For holding, loosening, tightening and turning of hex nuts and bolt or screw heads; usually offset for work on flat surfaces. Typically available in sets (different-sized box at each end) in lengths of 7 to 14 inches for gripping diameter of 1/4 to 1 inch.

Open-end wrenches
For holding and fast turning of hex or square nuts and bolts or screw heads. Typically available in sets (different-sized opening at each end) in lengths of 4 to 10 inches for gripping diameter of 1/4 to 1 inch.

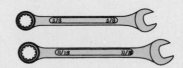

Combination wrenches
Open-end and box heads of same size at opposite ends for alternate use as open-end or box wrench. Typically available in sets in lengths of 4 to 17 inches for gripping diameter of 1/4 to 1 inch.

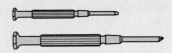
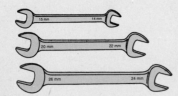

WRENCHES (continued)

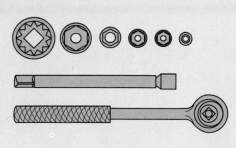

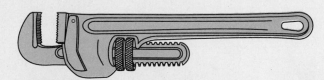

Ratchet socket wrench
For loosening, tightening and fast turning of hex or square nuts and bolt or screw heads. Typically available in sets: handle with ratchet mechanism and drive post of 3/8 inch for sockets from 3/8 to 1 inch; adapter for sockets from 1/8 to 1/4 inch; extension to lengthen reach of wrench.

Pipe wrench
For holding and turning of plumbing pipes and fittings; serrated jaws adjustable to range of opening widths (monkey wrench similar but without teeth). Typically available in lengths of 10 inches for gripping diameter of up to 1 1/2 inches; 14 inches for gripping diameter of up to 3 inches.

Strap wrench
For gripping and turning of plumbing pipes and fittings; strap of webbing material adjustable to range of opening widths and does not mar surface. Typically available with strap 12 inches in length.

Hex wrenches
Also known as Allen wrenches. For installing and removing screws with hex recesses. Typically available in sets to fit recesses of 5/64 to 1/4 inch.

PLIERS

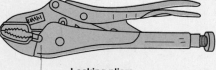

Slip-joint pliers
Also known as utility pliers. General-purpose tool for gripping, bending and turning. Serrated jaws adjustable to small and large opening widths. Usually available in lengths of 6 to 8 inches.

Channel-joint pliers
Also known as tongue-and-groove pliers. Heavy-duty, general-purpose tool for gripping, bending and turning. Serrated jaws adjustable to range of opening widths. Usually available in lengths of 7 to 16 inches.

Locking pliers
Also known as toggle-locking plier wrench. General-purpose tool for gripping, bending and turning. Serrated jaws locked when handles squeezed together; thumbscrew for adjusting locking width and release lever for opening. Usually available in lengths of 6 to 10 inches.

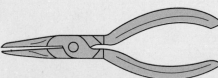

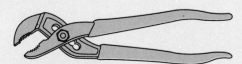

Long-nose pliers
Also known as needle-nose or thin-nose pliers. General-purpose tool for gripping and bending small objects, especially in restricted spaces; jaws incorporate wire cutter at joint. Usually available in lengths of 6 to 8 inches; types with curved nose also common.

Lineman's pliers
Heavy-duty, general-purpose tool for gripping, bending and cutting wires and cables. Serrated jaws incorporate wire cutter at joint. Usually available in lengths of 7 to 8 inches.

Diagonal-cutting pliers
Also known as side-cutting pliers or wire cutters. General-purpose tool for cutting wires and fasteners such as cotter pins, especially in restricted spaces; not suited for gripping or bending. Angled blades permit flush cuts. Usually available in lengths of 6 to 7 inches.

Snap-ring pliers
Also known as ring pliers. Specialty tool for removing and installing snap rings; different models for external and internal types of snap rings with interchangeable tips. Usually available in lengths of 5 to 12 inches; types with curved nose also common.

APPLICATING HAND TOOLS

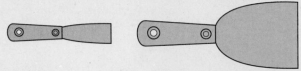

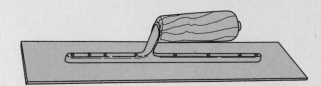

Putty knives
General-purpose tools for applying compounds or light scraping. Smaller type with flexible metal blade usually available in widths of 1 1/4 to 2 inches; larger type with stiff metal blade (also known as wall scraper) usually available in widths of 3 to 6 inches. Handle of plastic or wood.

Rectangular trowel
Also known as plasterer's trowel or metal float. General-purpose tool for applying compounds and leveling or smoothing. Rectangular metal blade typically 4 inches wide and 10 inches long. Handle of wood or plastic.

Joint filler
Also known as tuck-pointing trowel. Specialty tool for applying and packing mortar into joints and cracks. Narrow, stiff metal blade 5 to 12 inches long. Handle of wood or plastic.

Pointing and masonry trowels
Pointing trowel also known as buttering trowel; masonry trowel also known as brick trowel. Specialty tools for applying and packing mortar. Tapered, triangular metal blade: pointing trowel typically 4 1/2 to 7 inches long; masonry trowel typically 9 1/2 to 12 inches long. Handle of wood or plastic.

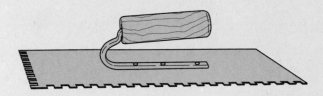

Notched trowel
Also known as adhesive trowel or mastic trowel. For applying and spreading adhesives (usually flooring types). Rectangular metal blade typically 4 1/2 inches wide and 9 1/2 inches long with notched edges; range of notch sizes for different adhesives. Handle of wood or plastic.

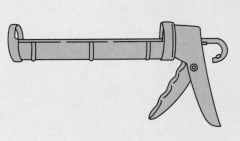

Paint roller
For applying paint, especially on large surfaces. Frame of plastic or metal with cover of synthetic fibers on cylinder of plastic (washable) or plasticized cardboard (disposable); handle threaded for extension handle. Covers typically available in lengths of 7 and 9 inches with various nap lengths: smooth (3/16 to 1/4 inch); medium (3/8 to 1/2 inch); rough (3/4 inch to 1 1/4 inches).

Caulking gun
For applying cartridge-type compounds, adhesives, sealants and caulks. Metal cylinder typically for cartridge of 10 1/2 ounces with ratchet or spring-pressure plunger action.

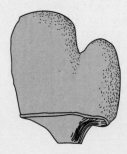

Paint mitt
For applying paint, especially on cylindrical or irregular-shaped surfaces. Mitt of synthetic or natural fibers with liner of plastic to prevent seepage.

Foam brush
For applying or touching-up paint, especially semi-gloss or gloss. Disposable foam pad on handle of plastic or wood.

Glue injector
For injecting continuous thin bead of adhesives. Plastic tube with syringe-like plunger action.

Paint pad
For applying paint, especially on large surfaces. Frame of plastic or metal with replaceable pad of synthetic fibers; fitted with handle of wood or plastic. Typically available in lengths of 7 to 10 inches.

Paintbrushes
For applying paint or other finish. Natural or synthetic bristles held by ferrule on handle of plastic or wood available in variety of styles and widths: trim or sash brush 1 inch to 2 inches wide typically for narrow surfaces; wall brush 3 to 5 inches wide typically for wide surfaces.

SCRAPING HAND TOOLS

Paint scraper
General-purpose tool for scraping, especially on flat surfaces. Handle of wood with replaceable 2- or 4-edged metal blades. Typically available in lengths of 6 to 14 inches with blades of 1 inch to 5 inches.

Wire brush
General-purpose tool for abrasive brushing, cleaning and scraping. Metal bristles embedded in handle of wood. Typically available in range of sizes and handle shapes.

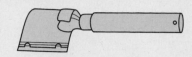

Razor-blade tool
General-purpose tool for light scraping or cutting. Handle usually of metal with single-edged retractable blade; typically available in range of styles.

Grout saw
For scraping grout out of joints between ceramic tiles (prior to regrouting). Palm-sized handle of plastic or wood with rough blade of tungsten carbide.

Window scraper
For scraping dried paint off glass. Handle of plastic or metal with retractable razor-type blade.

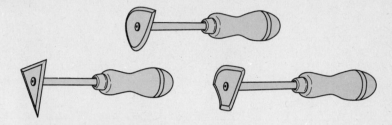

Molding scrapers
Also know as joint hooks. For removing chemical-or heat-softened finish: triangular-shaped blade for corners and grooves; teardrop-shaped blade for curves and contours; combination blade with triangular and teardrop shapes. Handles of wood or plastic.

Mortar hook
Also known as joint raker. For cleaning particles of mortar out of joints between masonry units (prior to repointing). Thin metal bar 14 to 16 inches long; typically available in range of end shapes.

Wall scrapers
General-purpose tools for light scraping or applying compounds. Larger type with stiff metal blade usually available in widths of 3 to 6 inches; smaller type with flexible metal blade (also known as putty knife) usually available in widths of 1 1/4 to 2 inches. Handle of plastic or wood.

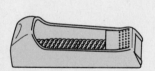

Surface-forming tool
For fast, rough trimming of wood, plastic or drywall. Available in different styles.

Sanding blocks
Hold sandpaper flat for smoothing wood surfaces and edges. Available in different styles made of metal, rubber or cork; homemade types using wood blocks or dowels can be customized.

PRYING HAND TOOLS

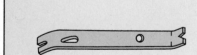

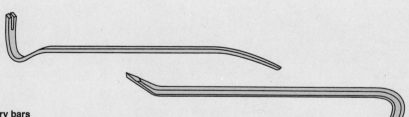

Utility bar
Prying tool for light jobs: pulling staples and small nails; lifting trim; prying lids of containers. Metal bar 8 inches long.

Pry bars
General-purpose prying tools for moderate to heavy jobs: pulling nails; prying apart joints. Standard pry bar of metal 12 to 24 inches long; wrecking bar (also known as crowbar) 24 inches long.

STAPLE GUN AND POP RIVETER

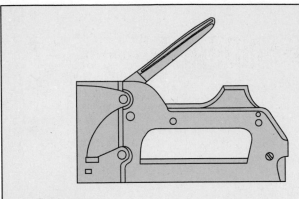

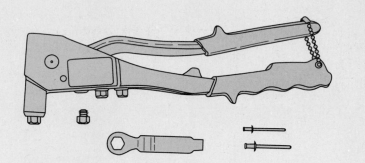

Staple gun
Special fastening tool for driving staples; heavy-duty type that can drive staples up to 9/16 inch long recommended. Slip-on attachments available for use in special jobs: tacking down electrical wires; stretching screening to fit across frame.

Pop riveter
Also known as rivet gun or riveter. Special fastening tool for driving pop rivets; interchangeable nosepieces for driving pop rivets from 3/32 to 3/16 inch in diameter. Available with long nose for extending reach in restricted spaces.

SOLDERING TOOLS

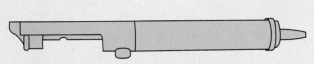

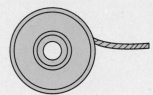

Desoldering braid
Braid of flux-coated copper wire for use with soldering iron to absorb solder residue or excess solder. Typically available in length of 5 feet on spool or bobbin in sizes No. 1 to No. 6.

Desoldering vacuum
Also known as solder sucker. For sucking up hot, melted solder when desoldering; spring-loaded plunger pushed down tube and released by pressing trigger.

Soldering iron
For heating and melting solder; typically available in power ratings of 15 to 40 watts for operating temperatures of 700 to 1,000° F. Interchangeable soldering tips of steel alloy coated with copper in various shapes and sizes: chisel or screwdriver type from 1/16 to 3/16 inch; conical type from 1/64 to 1/32 inch; precision point.

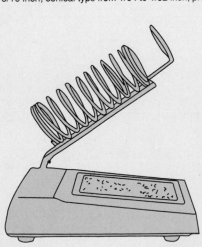

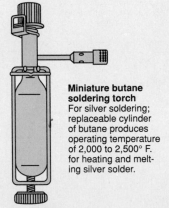

Miniature butane soldering torch
For silver soldering; replaceable cylinder of butane produces operating temperature of 2,000 to 2,500° F. for heating and melting silver solder.

Soldering iron stand
For holding soldering iron: coil of metal helps to dissipate heat and maintain even temperature; weighted base for storing moistened sponge to wipe off tip.

Propane torch
For sweat-soldering joints of copper pipes and fittings; replaceable canister of propane with screw-on nozzle. Canister of butane may be used to produce higher temperature.

PLUMBING PLUNGERS AND AUGERS

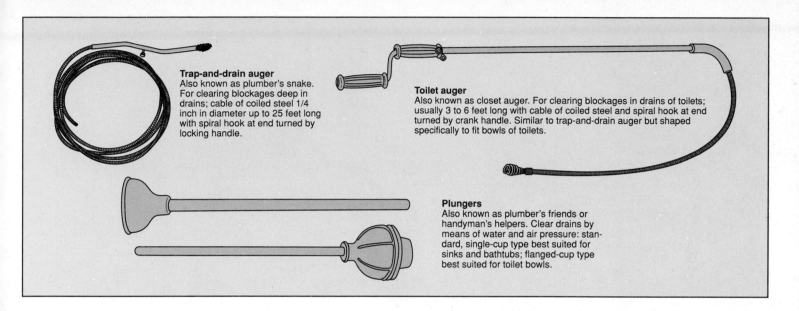

Trap-and-drain auger
Also known as plumber's snake. For clearing blockages deep in drains; cable of coiled steel 1/4 inch in diameter up to 25 feet long with spiral hook at end turned by locking handle.

Toilet auger
Also known as closet auger. For clearing blockages in drains of toilets; usually 3 to 6 feet long with cable of coiled steel and spiral hook at end turned by crank handle. Similar to trap-and-drain auger but shaped specifically to fit bowls of toilets.

Plungers
Also known as plumber's friends or handyman's helpers. Clear drains by means of water and air pressure: standard, single-cup type best suited for sinks and bathtubs; flanged-cup type best suited for toilet bowls.

ELECTRICAL TESTING TOOLS

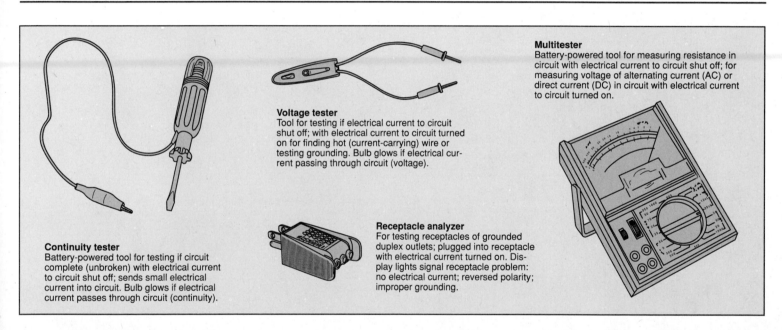

Multitester
Battery-powered tool for measuring resistance in circuit with electrical current to circuit shut off; for measuring voltage of alternating current (AC) or direct current (DC) in circuit with electrical current to circuit turned on.

Voltage tester
Tool for testing if electrical current to circuit shut off; with electrical current to circuit turned on for finding hot (current-carrying) wire or testing grounding. Bulb glows if electrical current passing through circuit (voltage).

Continuity tester
Battery-powered tool for testing if circuit complete (unbroken) with electrical current to circuit shut off; sends small electrical current into circuit. Bulb glows if electrical current passes through circuit (continuity).

Receptacle analyzer
For testing receptacles of grounded duplex outlets; plugged into receptacle with electrical current turned on. Display lights signal receptacle problem: no electrical current; reversed polarity; improper grounding.

EXTENSION CORDS

NAMEPLATE AMPS	2.0 to 6.0	6.1 to 10.0	10.1 to 12.0	12.1 to 15.0
EXTENSION CORD LENGTH	RECOMMENDED WIRE GAUGE (AWG)			
25 ft.	18	18	16	14
50 ft.	16	16	16	12
100 ft.	16	14	14	Not recommended
150 ft.	14	12	12	Not recommended

Reading the chart. An extension cord used with a tool must be of a suitable wire gauge. Find the amperage rating of the tool on its nameplate, then estimate the length of the extension cord needed and use the chart above to determine the wire gauge of the extension cord needed.

MEASURING AND MARKING TOOLS

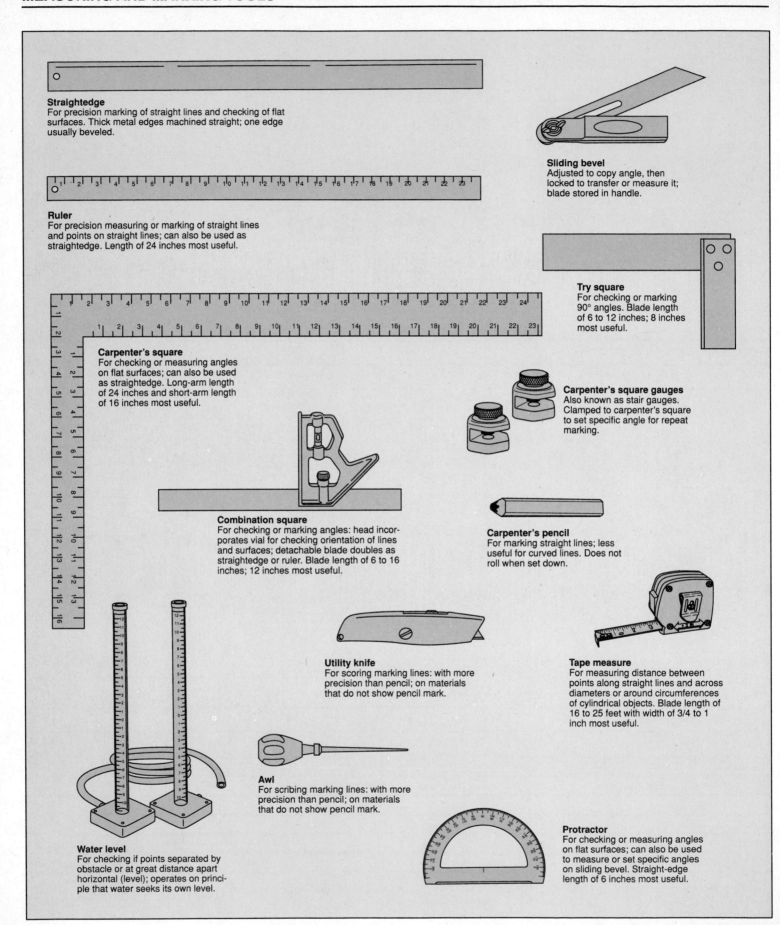

Straightedge
For precision marking of straight lines and checking of flat surfaces. Thick metal edges machined straight; one edge usually beveled.

Sliding bevel
Adjusted to copy angle, then locked to transfer or measure it; blade stored in handle.

Ruler
For precision measuring or marking of straight lines and points on straight lines; can also be used as straightedge. Length of 24 inches most useful.

Try square
For checking or marking 90° angles. Blade length of 6 to 12 inches; 8 inches most useful.

Carpenter's square
For checking or measuring angles on flat surfaces; can also be used as straightedge. Long-arm length of 24 inches and short-arm length of 16 inches most useful.

Carpenter's square gauges
Also known as stair gauges. Clamped to carpenter's square to set specific angle for repeat marking.

Combination square
For checking or marking angles: head incorporates vial for checking orientation of lines and surfaces; detachable blade doubles as straightedge or ruler. Blade length of 6 to 16 inches; 12 inches most useful.

Carpenter's pencil
For marking straight lines; less useful for curved lines. Does not roll when set down.

Utility knife
For scoring marking lines: with more precision than pencil; on materials that do not show pencil mark.

Tape measure
For measuring distance between points along straight lines and across diameters or around circumferences of cylindrical objects. Blade length of 16 to 25 feet with width of 3/4 to 1 inch most useful.

Awl
For scribing marking lines: with more precision than pencil; on materials that do not show pencil mark.

Water level
For checking if points separated by obstacle or at great distance apart horizontal (level); operates on principle that water seeks its own level.

Protractor
For checking or measuring angles on flat surfaces; can also be used to measure or set specific angles on sliding bevel. Straight-edge length of 6 inches most useful.

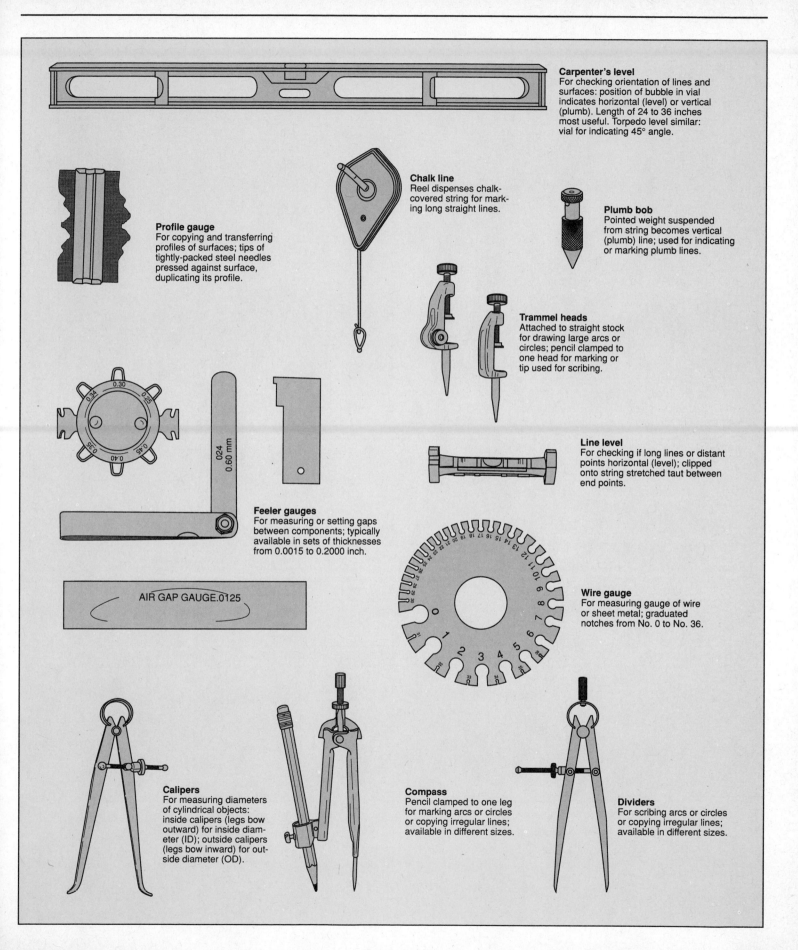

Carpenter's level
For checking orientation of lines and surfaces: position of bubble in vial indicates horizontal (level) or vertical (plumb). Length of 24 to 36 inches most useful. Torpedo level similar: vial for indicating 45° angle.

Chalk line
Reel dispenses chalk-covered string for marking long straight lines.

Plumb bob
Pointed weight suspended from string becomes vertical (plumb) line; used for indicating or marking plumb lines.

Profile gauge
For copying and transferring profiles of surfaces; tips of tightly-packed steel needles pressed against surface, duplicating its profile.

Trammel heads
Attached to straight stock for drawing large arcs or circles; pencil clamped to one head for marking or tip used for scribing.

Line level
For checking if long lines or distant points horizontal (level); clipped onto string stretched taut between end points.

Feeler gauges
For measuring or setting gaps between components; typically available in sets of thicknesses from 0.0015 to 0.2000 inch.

AIR GAP GAUGE.0125

Wire gauge
For measuring gauge of wire or sheet metal; graduated notches from No. 0 to No. 36.

Calipers
For measuring diameters of cylindrical objects: inside calipers (legs bow outward) for inside diameter (ID); outside calipers (legs bow inward) for outside diameter (OD).

Compass
Pencil clamped to one leg for marking arcs or circles or copying irregular lines; available in different sizes.

Dividers
For scribing arcs or circles or copying irregular lines; available in different sizes.

LADDERS

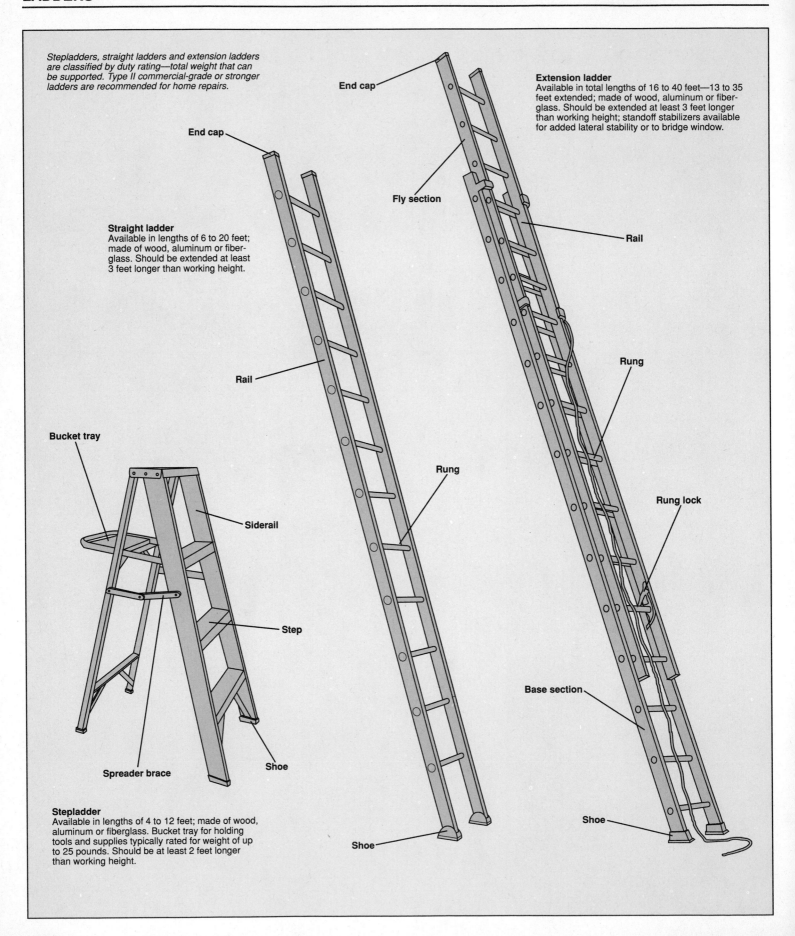

Stepladders, straight ladders and extension ladders are classified by duty rating—total weight that can be supported. Type II commercial-grade or stronger ladders are recommended for home repairs.

End cap

Straight ladder
Available in lengths of 6 to 20 feet; made of wood, aluminum or fiberglass. Should be extended at least 3 feet longer than working height.

Rail

Bucket tray

Siderail

Step

Spreader brace

Shoe

Stepladder
Available in lengths of 4 to 12 feet; made of wood, aluminum or fiberglass. Bucket tray for holding tools and supplies typically rated for weight of up to 25 pounds. Should be at least 2 feet longer than working height.

End cap

Rung

Shoe

Extension ladder
Available in total lengths of 16 to 40 feet—13 to 35 feet extended; made of wood, aluminum or fiberglass. Should be extended at least 3 feet longer than working height; standoff stabilizers available for added lateral stability or to bridge window.

Fly section

Rail

Rung

Rung lock

Base section

Shoe

SAWHORSES

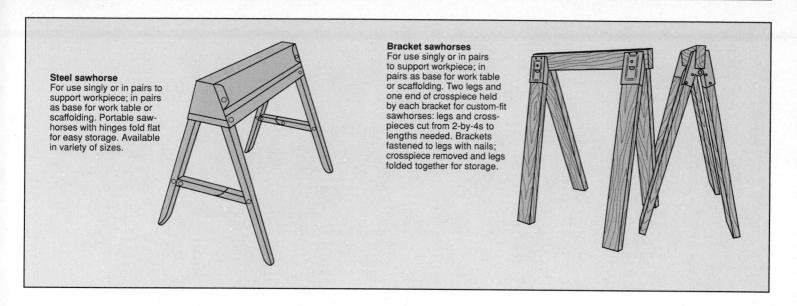

Steel sawhorse
For use singly or in pairs to support workpiece; in pairs as base for work table or scaffolding. Portable sawhorses with hinges fold flat for easy storage. Available in variety of sizes.

Bracket sawhorses
For use singly or in pairs to support workpiece; in pairs as base for work table or scaffolding. Two legs and one end of crosspiece held by each bracket for custom-fit sawhorses: legs and crosspieces cut from 2-by-4s to lengths needed. Brackets fastened to legs with nails; crosspiece removed and legs folded together for storage.

CLAMPS AND VISES

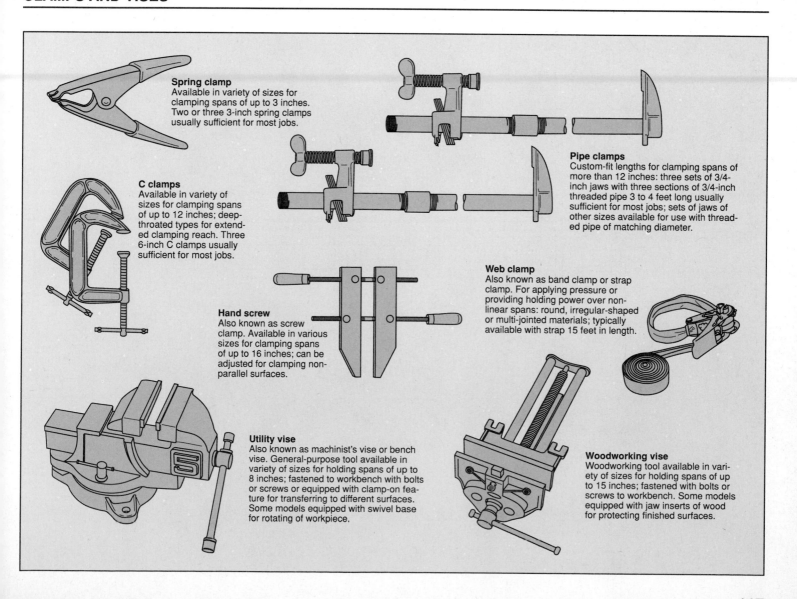

Spring clamp
Available in variety of sizes for clamping spans of up to 3 inches. Two or three 3-inch spring clamps usually sufficient for most jobs.

C clamps
Available in variety of sizes for clamping spans of up to 12 inches; deep-throated types for extended clamping reach. Three 6-inch C clamps usually sufficient for most jobs.

Pipe clamps
Custom-fit lengths for clamping spans of more than 12 inches: three sets of 3/4-inch jaws with three sections of 3/4-inch threaded pipe 3 to 4 feet long usually sufficient for most jobs; sets of jaws of other sizes available for use with threaded pipe of matching diameter.

Hand screw
Also known as screw clamp. Available in various sizes for clamping spans of up to 16 inches; can be adjusted for clamping non-parallel surfaces.

Web clamp
Also known as band clamp or strap clamp. For applying pressure or providing holding power over non-linear spans: round, irregular-shaped or multi-jointed materials; typically available with strap 15 feet in length.

Utility vise
Also known as machinist's vise or bench vise. General-purpose tool available in variety of sizes for holding spans of up to 8 inches; fastened to workbench with bolts or screws or equipped with clamp-on feature for transferring to different surfaces. Some models equipped with swivel base for rotating of workpiece.

Woodworking vise
Woodworking tool available in variety of sizes for holding spans of up to 15 inches; fastened with bolts or screws to workbench. Some models equipped with jaw inserts of wood for protecting finished surfaces.

DETECTORS AND ALARMS

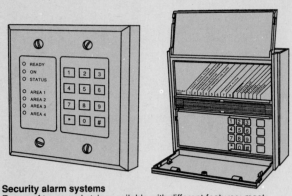

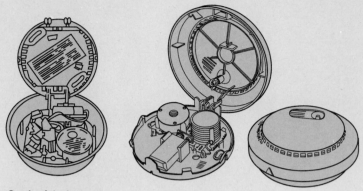

Security alarm systems
Range of types and styles available with different features; most sound alarm when presence of intruder detected—emitting loud noise from bell, siren or tone generator. Some types equipped with built-in strobe light that flashes when alarm sounds; some types also equipped with built-in fire sensor.

Smoke detectors
Battery-operated detectors sound alarm when smoke detected: ionization type that "senses" smoke; photoelectric type that "sees" smoke. Some models equipped with built-in light to illuminate escape route when alarm sounds; batteries should be tested monthly.

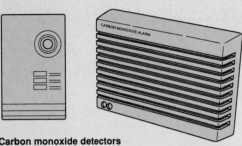

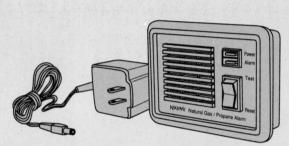

Carbon monoxide detectors
Passive-type detector with sensor darkens in color in response to rising levels of carbon monoxide in air; replaced annually or at expiry date. Battery-operated detector sounds when dangerous levels of carbon monoxide present in air; batteries should be tested monthly.

Radon gas detector
Kit with activated-charcoal detector for testing short-term concentration levels of radon gas in air; following test period, kit sent to certified laboratory for analysis and results.

Natural gas and propane gas detector
Plug-in detector sounds alarm when concentrations of natural gas or propane gas present in air; detector should be tested monthly.

FIRE EXTINGUISHERS

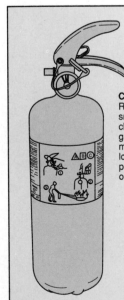

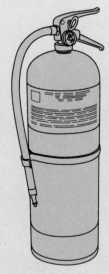

Class ABC
Rated effective against any small, contained fire; dry-chemical based. Pressure gauge should be checked monthly; after discharge or loss of pressure, must be professionally recharged or replaced.

Class A
Rated effective only against small, contained fire in ordinary combustibles—including wood, paper, cloth, rubber and many plastics; water or chemical based. Cannot be used to extinguish class B or C fire. Pressure gauge should be checked monthly; after discharge or loss of pressure, must be professionally recharged or replaced.

Class BC
Rated effective only against small, contained fire in flammable liquid or electrical unit; carbon-dioxide or halon based and may be equipped with horn to protect skin from cold temperature of discharge. Cannot be used to extinguish class A fire. Pressure gauge should be checked monthly; after discharge or loss of pressure, must be professionally recharged or replaced.

PERSONAL SAFETY EQUIPMENT

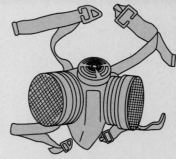

Safety goggles
Typically of flexible, molded plastic: type with perforated vent holes for eye protection from impact injury; type with baffled vents for eye protection from chemical injury; type without vents for eye protection from irritating dust or fumes.

Disposable dust mask
Filter of cotton fiber or gauze with foam seal and metal nose clip; adjustable head straps. Provides single-use protection against inhalation of nuisance dust or mist.

Reusable dust mask
Frame of neoprene rubber or soft plastic with adjustable head strap and disposable filter of cotton fiber or gauze. Permits repeated-use protection against inhalation of nuisance dust or mist.

Dual-cartridge respirator
Frame of neoprene rubber or soft plastic with adjustable head straps; fitted with interchangeable cartridges and/or filters for protection against inhalation of specific dust, mist or vapor toxic hazard. Provides purifying of air as inhaled through filters and/or cartridges; expelling of contaminated air through exhalation valve.

Cotton gloves
Typically of 8- to 10-ounce cotton. For use alone for light-duty handling of tools and materials; for use over rubber gloves for work with abrasives and chemicals.

Work gloves
Typically of leather or thick fabric with leather palms and fingertips; elasticized or knitted wrists. For use for heavy-duty handling of rough or sharp tools and materials.

Rubber gloves
Household rubber gloves or disposable vinyl gloves for work with mild chemicals; neoprene rubber gloves for work with harsh chemicals.

Safety helmet
Typically of reinforced plastic with adjustable head strap. Provides protection against impact injury to head when working overhead or in restricted space with little headroom.

Ear muffs
Cushioned muffs with adjustable head strap of flexible plastic; head strap can be worn over or behind head or under chin. Provide repeated-use hearing protection against high-intensity noise of power tools and equipment.

Ear plugs
Typically of foam; compressed and inserted into ear canals, then allowed to expand to fit shape of ear canals. Provide single-use hearing protection against high-intensity noise of power tools and equipment.

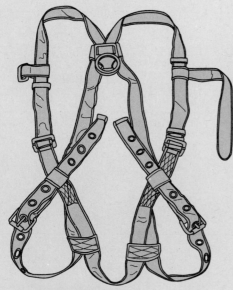

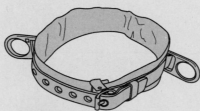

Lanyard
Rope 5/8 inch thick or webbing of nylon 4 to 8 feet long with locking hook on each end; clips onto metal ring of safety harness or belt and onto rope grab.

Safety harness
Fully-adjustable body harness usually made of nylon. Provides protection against fall from roof; metal ring on back attached to fall-arrest system: lanyard, rope grab and fall-arrest rope. Available in waist sizes from small (32 to 40 inches) to extra-large (44 to 52 inches).

Safety belt
Adjustable belt usually made of nylon. Substitute for safety harness in providing protection against fall from roof: metal ring over hip attached to fall-arrest system: lanyard, rope grab and fall-arrest rope. Available in waist sizes from small (32 to 40 inches) to extra-large (44 to 52 inches).

Rope grab
Mechanism of stainless steel or aluminum attached to lanyard and to fall-arrest rope (tied to sturdy, fixed object on ground). Permits controlled movement up and down on fall-arrest rope, but locks instantly if jerked suddenly.

FIRST AID SUPPLIES

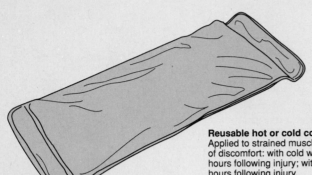

Reusable hot or cold compress
Applied to strained muscles or joints for relief of discomfort: with cold water (or ice) up to 48 hours following injury; with hot water after 48 hours following injury.

Reusable ice pack
Filled with ice and applied to strained muscles or joints for relief of discomfort up to 48 hours following injury.

Gauze roller bandage
Sterile roll for securing gauze dressings; secured with medical tape or safety pin or by knotting. Available in lengths of 5 to 10 yards in widths of 1 inch to 4 inches.

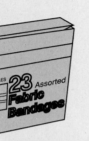

Adhesive bandages
Sterile gauze dressings with adhesive strips for protecting scratches or minor cuts. Available in variety of sizes and shapes: rectangular, square, round, butterfly and fingertip.

Gauze dressing
Sterile pad for covering wound; secured with medical tape or gauze roller bandage. Available in sizes of 2-by-2 inches, 3-by-3 inches and 4-by-4 inches.

Medical tape
For securing gauze dressings, gauze roller bandages or eye pads; hypo-allergenic for sensitive skin. Available in lengths of 2 1/2 to 10 yards in widths of 1/2 inch to 3 inches.

Triangular bandage
Multipurpose cotton bandage can be folded to make sling, swath, ring pad or head bandage; measures 55 inches across base and 36 to 40 inches along each side.

Elasticized roller bandage
Roll of woven cotton and rubber for applying compression to strained muscles or joints; secured with clips of metal or plastic. Available in lengths of 10 feet in widths of 2 to 6 inches.

Eye pads
Sterile pads taped loosely over eyes to protect them and prevent movement; also available as oval-shaped, self-adhering patches.

Eye irrigator
Filled with water and used to flush foreign particle out of eye.

Tweezers
For extracting splinter or other small object embedded in skin. Of stainless steel in variety of shapes and sizes; flat-tipped type 4 1/2 inches long common.

Rubbing alcohol
Also known as isopropyl alcohol; for sterilizing tweezers and other first-aid equipment.

Hydrogen peroxide
Commonly available in 3% solution; for cleaning wounds before applying adhesive bandages, gauze dressings or gauze roller bandages.

Petroleum jelly
For moisturizing dry, chapped skin.

Calamine lotion
Zinc oxide compound for soothing minor skin irritation from poisonous plant or insect bite; hydrocortizone cream can also be used.

Cotton balls
For applying soothing medication such as calamine lotion or hydrocortizone cream to minor skin irritation.

Ipecac syrup
For inducing vomiting in victim of poisoning. **Caution:** Administer only if advised by poison control center or physician.

Thermometer
Calibrated vial filled with mercury for determining body temperature: oral type for adult or child; rectal type for infant. Newer electronic models give temperature reading on liquid crystal display (LCD).

Medicine spoon
Calibrated plastic tube for administering precise dosage of liquid medication.

Medicine dropper
Calibrated plastic tube with rubber bulb for administering precise dosage of liquid medication to infant.

CHILD SAFETY DEVICES

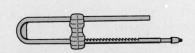

Cabinet lock
U-shaped bar fitted around or behind handles of twin doors; held in place by button-activated clip that slides onto bar and locks in place.

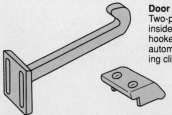

Door safety latch
Two-piece lock mounted with screws inside cupboard, closet or cabinet; hooked latch fastened to door locks automatically in place behind retaining clip fastened to inside surface.

Doorknob cover
Fitted onto doorknob to prevent opening of door; round disk placed behind doorknob and cup-shaped cover locked into it over doorknob.

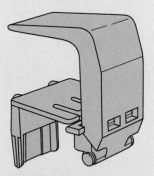

Toilet lid lock
Hinged lock attached to lip of toilet bowl with adjustable clamp. Locking arm raised into place over toilet lid and held in place by clips; cannot be lowered unless release latches lifted.

Refrigerator lock
Two-piece device for holding door of refrigerator closed; tab attached to door and latch mounted on adjacent surface to automatically lock on it when door closed.

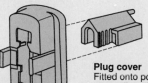

Plug cover
Fitted onto post screwed to cover plate of duplex outlet, concealing plug and its prongs; prevents children from tampering with plug. Released by spreading tabs and pulling off post.

Safety caps
Fitted into slots of unused receptacle in outlet to prevent children from inserting fingers or objects; protects against electrical shock.

GLOSSARY

A

A Grade rating of the face or back of a plywood panel; indicates the surface is smooth and paintable.

ABC Effectiveness rating of a fire extinguisher: A and B ratings indicate effectiveness against fires of combustible solids and flammable liquids; C rating indicates effectiveness against fires of electrical tools, appliances and systems.

Abrasive Substance (usually sandpaper or steel wool) used to remove material from a surface by scraping or friction.

AC Abbreviation of alternating current, where the flow of electrons is in both directions; the electrical system of a household provides this type of electricity.

Actual size Term used to specify the size of lumber after drying and surfacing.

Air-dried lumber Lumber that has been piled to dry in the air for a length of time, leaving it with a moisture content of 12 to 15% or higher.

Air-entrained concrete Concrete treated with an additive to create microscopic air bubbles that cushion the effects of water expansion and contraction; reduces damage from freeze-thaw cycles and deicing salts.

Al Abbreviation of the element aluminum; often marked on wires and other units made of aluminum.

Alligatoring Splitting up of a paint or other finish into segments; occurs when a new coat does not adhere to the old coat.

Ampacity Maximum current-carrying capacity of a wire; measured in amperes.

Ampere Unit of measurement for the amount of current passing through a point at a given time. To calculate wattage, multiply amperes by voltage (120 or 240).

Annual Flower that grows from seed, blooms and dies in one season.

Area To calculate the area for a square, square the length of one side; for a rectangle, multiply the length by the width; for a circle, square the radius and multiply by 3.14.

AWG Abbreviation of American Wire Gauge, a measurement standard of the diameter or thickness of metal: wire, cable, sheet metal, for example.

B

B Grade rating of the face or back of a plywood panel; indicates the surface may have tight knots up to 1 inch wide and minor splits.

Back-siphonage Reverse flow of water (possibly contaminated) into supply pipes of the plumbing system: from a bathtub, sink, swimming pool, for example.

Bevel cut Type of wood cut; a cut usually at a 45° angle through the thickness or along the length of a piece. *See wood cuts; chart, below.*

Bevel joint Type of wood joint; the ends of two pieces fitted together at an angle usually of 45°, concealing the end grain. *See wood joints; chart, page 123.*

Blind-nail To drive in a nail at a 45° angle through the tongue of a board for concealing by the groove of the next board: in wood siding, wood flooring, for example.

Board foot Standard measurement unit of lumber: 1 board foot is the equivalent of a nominal size 1-by-12 (1 inch thick by 12 inches wide) 1 foot long. To calculate board feet, multiply the number of pieces by the nominal thickness (inches) and the nominal width (inches), then multiply by the length (feet) and divide by 12.

Board lumber Lumber dried and cut to standard sizes less than 2 inches thick and 2 or more inches wide.

Bonding Joining of materials; usually by using an adhesive.

Bore To drill a hole in wood.

Branch circuit Wiring that carries current away from and back to the main service panel—running between the main service panel and a series of outlets, wall switches, light fixtures, for example.

Brick cube Prepackaged set of bricks.

Btu Abbreviation of British thermal unit, a measurement unit of heat energy: the approximate equivalent of the heat given off by burning one wooden match. To convert from Btus to watt-hours, divide by 3.413.

Butt joint Type of wood joint; the end of one piece fitted against the side or end of another piece without overlapping. *See wood joints; chart, page 123.*

Butt line Line formed by the edge-to-edge alignment of a row of units: shakes, shingles, for example.

Butted seam Edge-to-edge joint without overlap; in a wallcovering, for example.

Buttering Applying of mortar or adhesive to the surface of a unit.

C

C Grade rating of the face or back of a plywood panel; indicates the surface may have tight knots up to 1 1/2 inches wide, knotholes up to 1 inch wide and limited splits.

C plugged Grade rating of the face or back of a plywood panel; indicates the surface may have filled knotholes up to 1/4-by-1/2 inch and splits up to 1/8 inch wide.

Caustic warning A triangle with a hand and a test tube warns that the product contains a substance which can burn the skin or eyes. *See chemical product safety symbols; chart, page 124.*

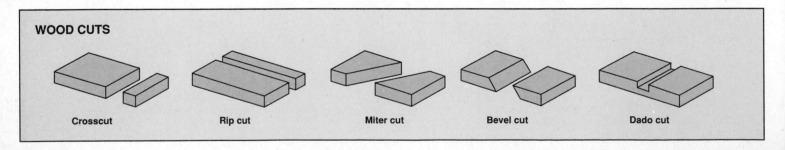

WOOD CUTS

| Crosscut | Rip cut | Miter cut | Bevel cut | Dado cut |

Chamfer Type of wood cut; a bevel usually of 45° along the edge of a piece.

Check Defect in wood that is characterized by splitting; caused by uneven drying.

Chipboard Type of board product that is manufactured by compressing together wood particles and glue into a mat.

Circuit Continuous path for current; in the electrical system of a household, a branch circuit starts from the main service panel, runs to a series of outlets, wall switches and light fixtures, and returns back to the main service panel.

Circuit overload Condition that occurs when the combination of electrical loads or demands on a circuit calls for more amperes than it is designed to handle.

Cleat Strip of wood used to support another piece: shelves, cabinets, for example.

Closed-coat sandpaper Sandpaper with closely-spaced abrasive particles.

Coarse aggregate Small stones added to a mix of concrete to provide bulk.

Coarse-textured wood Wood with large pores; also known as open-grained wood.

Continuity Describes a circuit that is complete or closed, having the potential to route current; can be tested for using a continuity tester or a multitester.

Coped end End of a piece cut with a coping saw; usually the end of a piece of trim for fitting with another piece of trim at a corner.

Corbeling Offsetting courses usually of bricks to create a stepped effect.

Counterbore To drill a hole in wood for the head of a screw or bolt to be seated below the surface (and be concealed by a wood plug, for example).

Counterflashing Second layer of flashing.

Countersink To drill a hole in wood for the head of a screw or bolt to be seated flush with the surface.

Course Continuous row of units: bricks, slates, floorboards, for example.

Cove Type of wood cut; often used for trim pieces. Also known as quarter-hollow cut.

CPR Abbreviation of cardiopulmonary resuscitation, a first-aid technique for reviving a person who has no pulse.

CPU Abbreviation of central processing unit, a silicon microchip that controls the functions of a computer.

Crazing Fine cracking of a paint or other finish or of a material such as concrete.

Cross grain Grain of a piece that runs at an angle to the dominant pattern (usually at an angle to the length).

Crosscut Type of wood cut; a straight cut across the grain of a piece (usually across the width). *See wood cuts; chart, page 122.*

CRT Abbreviation of cathode ray tube, the picture tube of a television or monitor of a computer.

Cu (or Co) Abbreviation of the element copper; often marked on wires and other units made of copper.

Cupping Curling at the edges along the length of a piece; in wood, caused by uneven shrinkage.

Cure To harden by chemical reaction (rather than set by drying or evaporation).

Current Flow of electricity: the movement of electrons, measured in amperes.

Cutting in Applying paint or other finish along the edges of a surface, usually at the inside corners.

D

D Grade rating of the back of a plywood panel; indicates the surface may have knots or knotholes up to 2 1/2 inches wide and limited splits.

d Symbol for penny, the standard measurement unit in the penny rating of nails.

Dado cut Type of wood cut; a groove or channel cut across the width or along the length of a piece. *See wood cuts; chart, page 122.*

Dado joint Type of wood joint; the end of one piece fitted into the groove or channel (dado) in another piece. *See wood joints; chart, below.*

Damper Adjustable metal plate of a fireplace that controls the amount of air flowing up the chimney.

WOOD JOINTS

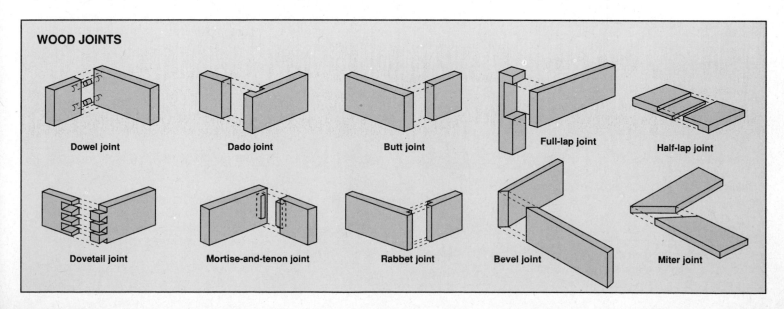

Dowel joint   Dado joint   Butt joint   Full-lap joint   Half-lap joint

Dovetail joint   Mortise-and-tenon joint   Rabbet joint   Bevel joint   Miter joint

DC Abbreviation of direct current, where the flow of electrons is in one direction; batteries provide this type of electricity.

Diameter Greatest distance between two points of a circle; equal to the length of a straight line through the center between two points of the circle.

Dimension lumber Lumber dried and cut to standard sizes from 2 up to less than 5 inches thick and 2 or more inches wide.

Double-insulated Describes a power tool with a non-conductive housing of plastic; provides protection for the user from an electrical shock.

Dovetail joint Type of wood joint; fingers and slots at the ends of two pieces fitted together. *See wood joints; chart, page 123.*

Dowel joint Type of wood joint; round pegs fitted into holes in the ends of two pieces. *See wood joints; chart, page 123.*

Dressed lumber Lumber with at least one surface planed smooth.

Dry-bonding Laying a practice run of bricks or blocks without mortar.

Dry-fitting Assembling a piece without gluing or permanent fastening.

DWV Abbreviation of drain-waste-vent, the drainage system for the plumbing system of a household.

E

Efflorescence White, powdery deposits often found on masonry; caused by the leaching of mineral salts.

EIM Abbreviation of electronic ignition module, a component of the ignition system for a power tool.

End grain Edge of a piece that is exposed after cutting across the grain.

End-of-the-run Describes an outlet or wall switch with only one cable entering the electrical box; the last electrical box of a branch circuit.

Etching Abrading of a surface by chemical action, usually in preparation for resurfacing or finishing; the treating of concrete with muriatic acid before the application of paint, for example.

Explosive warning A triangle with an exploding object warns that the container of the product may explode if it is heated or punctured. *See chemical product safety symbols; chart, below.*

F

Face-nail To drive in a nail straight through the face of a piece, securing it to a parallel piece or surface: in wood siding, wood flooring, for example.

Feathering Thinning and tapering the edges of a compound to blend with the surrounding surface: in patching, for example.

Fence Adjustable guide that keeps the cutting edge of a tool in a set position, usually in relation to the edge of a workpiece.

Fillet Thin strip of wood.

Firestop Block of 2-by-4 installed horizontally between two studs; helps to retard the spread of a fire.

FIZZBO Acronym for the phrase "for sale by owner," referring to the homeowner who is selling his house without the services of a real estate agent.

Flammable warning A triangle with flames warns that the product contains a flammable substance. *See chemical product safety symbols; chart, below.*

Flange Projecting ridge or collar that provides a unit with rigidity or permits it to be fastened.

Flux Substance applied to a metal surface to clean it before soldering.

CHEMICAL PRODUCT SAFETY SYMBOLS

Poison warning

Caustic warning

Flammable warning

Explosive warning

Frost line Deepest penetration of frost below ground level.

Full-lap joint Type of wood joint; full width and thickness of one piece fitted into dado of another piece. *See wood joints; chart, page 123.*

G

Gauge Diameter or thickness of a unit, usually a standard measure: screws, wires, sheet metal, for example.

Gooseneck Section of a balustrade connecting the handrail and the upper newel post, for example.

gph Abbreviation of gallons per hour, a measurement of the firing rate of the nozzle on an oil burner.

Grade Term most commonly used to indicate the quality of wood.

Grain Dominant direction of fibers in wood.

Green lumber Freshly-cut wood that has not been purposely dried; usually has a moisture content of 30% or more.

Groove Type of wood cut; a channel cut across the width or along the length of a piece, often on the edge for fitting with a tongue: in wood siding, wood flooring, for example.

Ground Connection between a circuit or electrical equipment and the earth.

Grounding wire Protective bare copper or green-insulated wire that drains off any current escaping its normal path to the main service panel.

H

Half-lap joint Type of wood joint; ends of two pieces with opposite half laps fitted together. *See wood joints; chart, page 123.*

Hardwood Lumber that is cut from (primarily) species of deciduous trees.

Header Horizontal wood support used to reinforce a framing opening: door, window, stairs, for example. Also, a brick with the short face (width) exposed.

Heartwood Mature wood found at the center of a tree.

Hg Abbreviation of the element mercury.

Hone To sharpen the cutting edge of a blade; to rub the blade of a chisel on an abrasive stone, for example.

Hot wire Wire that carries current from an electrical source; typically identified by black or red insulation.

Housing Covering for internal components; also a dado for fitting a dovetail tenon, tread, shelf, for example.

I-J

IC Abbreviation of integrated circuit, a type of circuitry used in electronic equipment.

ID Abbreviation of inside diameter.

Jig Device for securing a tool or workpiece to permit the repetition of a procedure.

K

Kerf Width of a cut in wood made by the blade of a saw.

Keyway Space or gap between rows of units: shakes, shingles, for example. Also, the groove for a key in a shaft, pulley, gear or sprocket of a power transmission.

Kiln-dried lumber Lumber that has been dried in a kiln; usually has a moisture content of 6 to 12%.

kwh Abbreviation of kilowatt hour, the standard measurement unit for consumption of electrical energy.

L

Laminate Thin strips of wood or plastic glued together.

Laser warning A triangle or square with a sunburst symbol warns of possible danger from a laser: in a compact disc player, for example. *See electronic safety symbols; chart, below.*

LCD Abbreviation of liquid-crystal display, a type of display used in electronic equipment.

LED Abbreviation of light-emitting diode, a type of display used in electronic equipment.

Level Perfectly horizontal.

Lintel Load-bearing horizontal support above a wall opening.

Long grain Grain of a piece that runs parallel to the dominant pattern (usually parallel to the length).

Lumber Wood of standard widths and thicknesses in common lengths that has been cut and planed but not otherwise processed.

M

Mastic Type of viscous adhesive.

Metric system System of measurement used by many countries. *See metric conversion; table, below.*

Middle-of-the-run Describes an outlet or wall switch with two cables entering the electrical box; other than the last electrical box of a branch circuit.

Millwork Wood produced for decorative trim.

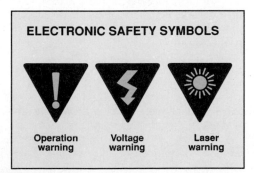

ELECTRONIC SAFETY SYMBOLS

| Operation warning | Voltage warning | Laser warning |

U.S. AND METRIC CONVERSION
To find the metric measure equivalent of a U.S. measure in the left column, multiply by the conversion factor in the center column. To find the U.S. measure equivalent of a metric measure in the right column, divide by the conversion factor in the center.

U.S. MEASURE	CONVERSION FACTOR	METRIC MEASURE
LINEAR		
Mile	1.609	Kilometer
Yard	0.9144	Meter
Foot	30.48	Centimeter
Inch	2.54	Centimeter
WEIGHT		
Ton	0.907	Metric ton
Pound	0.454	Kilogram
Ounce	28.350	Gram
VOLUME (LIQUID)		
Gallon	3.785	Liter
Quart	0.946	Liter
Pint	0.473	Liter
Fluidounce	29.573	Milliliter
VOLUME (DRY)		
Bushel	35.239	Liter
Peck	8.810	Liter
Quart	1.101	Liter
Pint	0.551	Liter
Cup	0.237	Liter
Ounce	0.167	Milliliter
Tablespoon	15.0	Milliliter
Teaspoon	5.0	Milliliter

Miter cut Type of wood cut; a cut usually at a 45° angle across the width of a piece. *See wood cuts; chart, page 122.*

Miter joint Type of wood joint; the ends of two pieces fitted together at an angle usually of 45°, concealing the end grain. *See wood joints; chart, page 123.*

Mortise-and-tenon joint Type of wood joint; projection (tenon) at end of one piece fitted into recess (mortise) in end of another piece. *See wood joints; chart, page 123.*

N

Neutral wire Wire that carries current back to an electrical source; typically identified by white insulation.

Nominal size Term used to specify the size of lumber before drying and surfacing.

NRR Abbreviation of noise reduction rating; a measurement in decibels of the effectiveness of hearing protection equipment.

O

OC Abbreviation of on center; describes the distance between the centers of supports: studs, joists, for example.

OD Abbreviation of outside diameter.

Ohm Unit of measurement for the amount of resistance in a circuit; can be measured with a multitester.

Open-coat sandpaper Sandpaper with widely-spaced abrasive particles.

Operation warning A triangle with an exclamation mark warns the user to consult the owner's manual before operating the unit. *See electronic safety symbols; chart, page 125.*

Outgassing Leaching of formaldehyde into the air from a product: plastic foam insulation, for example.

Overlap joint Type of wood joint; end of one piece fitted against side of another piece and may be butted against end of third piece.

P

Parging Covering of a masonry wall with a thin coat of mortar.

Particle board Type of board product manufactured by bonding together flakes or chips of wood and glue under pressure.

Patina Visible hue and texture that develops in finished wood as it ages.

Penny rating Standard measurement for the length of nails; originally referred to the price per 100 nails. One penny (penny-weight unit) is approximately the equivalent of 0.05 ounce or 1.555 grams.

Perennial Flower with a root system that survives a period of dormancy and blooms each year.

pH Logarithmic scale used for measuring the acidity or alkalinity of a substance: soil, for example. Runs from 0 to 14 with 7 as neutral: 6 to 0 indicates range of acidity; 8 to 14 indicates range of alkalinity.

Pilot hole Small hole bored or drilled for guiding a fastener, usually a screw or a nail; of diameter smaller than the shank.

Plug Cylindrical-shaped piece of sod about 2 1/2 inches in diameter and 2 inches thick; obtained by cutting a section of established lawn using a plug-cutting tool or bulb planter.

Plumb Perfectly vertical.

Plywood Type of board product manufactured by bonding together three or more layers of thin wood under pressure, with alternating layers usually running at right angles to each other.

Pointing Replacing the mortar of the joints between bricks or other masonry units; also called repointing or tuck-pointing.

Poison warning A triangle with a skull and crossbones warns that the product contains a substance which is poisonous if ingested or inhaled. *See chemical product safety symbols; chart, page 124.*

Primer Undercoat of paint or sealer applied to seal an unfinished surface and provide a base for finish coats of paint or other finish.

psi Abbreviation of pounds per square inch, a standard measurement unit of pressure: water, air, for example.

Q-R

Quarter-round Type of wood cut; often used for trim pieces.

R-value Standard measurement unit for the resistance of heat flow through a material; most commonly expressed as resistance per inch of material. Runs from R-0 to R-8, with the higher numerical value indicating higher insulating properties.

Rabbet joint Type of wood joint; steps in ends of two pieces fitted together. *See wood joints; chart, page 123.*

Ratchet Part with teeth that engages a cog or pin to confine motion in one direction.

Refractory cement Cement specially formulated to withstand high temperature; used to cast firebricks, for example.

Refrigerant A compressible heat-transfer substance that absorbs and radiates heat: in air conditioners, refrigerators, for example.

Rip cut Type of wood cut; a straight cut along the grain of a piece (usually along the length). *See wood cuts; chart, page 122.*

rpm Abbreviation of revolutions per minute, a measurement of turning speed.

S

SAE Abbreviation of Society of Automotive Engineers, an organization advancing elements of the design and construction of automotive equipment. SAE rating of viscosity appears on the labels of automotive oil products, for example.

Sand paint Paint mixed with sand to produce a rough-textured finish: on exterior stairs, for example.

Scoring Marking a line along a surface using a cutting or scribing tool: utility knife, awl, for example.

Seasoning Reducing the moisture content of wood by kiln- or air-drying.

Self-tapping screw Screw that is used to fasten metal; the shank of the screw cuts threads in the metal as it is driven into a pilot hole.

Selvage Blank strip: at the edge of carpeting, resilient flooring, wallcovering, for example.

Set Term that refers to the bend in the teeth of a blade, the angle between the teeth and the main axis of the blade. Tooth set allows a blade to cut a kerf slightly wider than itself to help prevent it from binding.

TEMPERATURE CONVERSION

To find the degrees Celcius (°C.) equivalent of degrees Farenheit (°F.), locate the numerical value of the temperature in the center column and refer to the corresponding entry in the left column. To find the °F. equivalent of °C., locate the numerical value of the temperature in the center column and refer to the corresponding entry in the right column.

°C (CELSIUS)		°F (FAHRENHEIT)
-29	**-20**	-4
-23	**-10**	14
-18	**0**	32
-12	**10**	50
-7	**20**	68
-1	**30**	86
4	**40**	104
10	**50**	122
16	**60**	140
21	**70**	158
24	**75**	167
27	**80**	176
29	**85**	185
32	**90**	194
35	**95**	203
37	**98**	203
38	**100**	212
43	**110**	230

Setscrew Screw without a head used to fasten parts of metal together: handles to faucets, for example.

sfpm Abbreviation of surface feet per minute, a measurement of speed; used for belt sanders, for example.

Shank Cylindrical shaft of a fastener, usually a nail or screw. Also, the straight part of a tool nearest the handle.

Shim Small, thin, usually tapered piece of wood, plastic or cardboard; used to fill gaps, align uneven surfaces, for example.

Shoring wall Temporary floor-to-ceiling frame of 2-by-4s.

Short circuit Condition that occurs when an exposed hot wire touches a neutral wire or a grounded electrical box, causing the circuit to heat up suddenly, for example.

Short grain Dominant grain that runs across a narrow piece.

Skew-nail To drive in nails at opposite angles through the face of a piece; provides greater holding power than face-nailing when securing a piece to a parallel piece or surface.

Softwood Lumber that is cut from (primarily) species of coniferous trees.

Sprig Individual grass plant 1 inch to 2 inches high with a few tufts of leaves; obtained by carefully pulling apart a section of sod from another area of lawn.

Stopped mortise Mortise that bottoms out in a piece; also called a stub mortise.

Straight grain Grain that runs parallel to the long edge of a piece.

Stretcher Brick with the long face (length) exposed.

Stub tenon Tenon that bottoms out in a stopped (or stub) mortise.

Surround Veneer covering on the bricks between the mantel and the opening of a fireplace.

Switch loop Circuit that serves only a switch.

T

Temperature Measured on two common scales: Fahrenheit (°F.) and Celsius (°C.). *See temperature conversion; table, left.*

Template Pattern or mold used as a guide to shape or form a piece.

Tenon Projection or tongue of a piece, usually for fitting into a mortise of another piece.

Test-fitting Testing the fit of a piece before gluing or permanent fastening.

Thatch Layer of roots, stems and runners of grass that develops between the leaf blades of a lawn and the soil.

Thinner Substance that can reduce the consistency of paint or other finish.

Toe-nail To drive in a nail at an angle through the face of a piece to secure it to a perpendicular piece or surface.

Tongue-and-groove joint Type of wood joint; a projecting ridge (tongue) along the edge of one piece fitted into the slot (groove) along the edge of another piece: wood siding, wood flooring, for example.

Tooling Leaving the impression of a finishing tool in a mortar joint.

Tooth Slightly roughened surface for a fresh coat of paint.

Traveler wire Wire connecting two or more switches that can each control the same circuit independently.

U-V-W

UHF Abbreviation of ultra high frequency, describing a range of television broadcasting signals.

Undercutting Cutting along under the inside edges of a crack or hole, producing a V-shaped opening to help grip or lock patching compound.

Veneer Thin sheet of wood (usually of high-quality hardwood).

VHF Abbreviation of very high frequency, describing a range of television broadcasting signals.

Viscosity Capacity of a liquid to flow.

Volt Unit of measurement for the pressure of current; circuits of the electrical system of a household are usually wired for 120 volts, 240 volts or low-voltage.

Voltage warning A triangle with a lightning bolt warns of a potential electrical shock hazard. *See electronic safety symbols; chart, page 125.*

Volume To calculate the volume of a rectangular-shaped solid, multiply the length by the width by the height.

Volute Spiral end on the handrail of a balustrade, for example.

Watt Unit of measurement for the rate of consumption of current. To calculate amperes, divide wattage by voltage (120 or 240).

Wet-sanding Smoothing using sandpaper with a waterproof backing and water; avoids clogging of the sandpaper.

ACKNOWLEDGMENTS

The editors wish to thank the following:
American Plywood Association, Tacoma, WA.; Sari Berger, Montreal, Que.; Camcar Textron, Rockford, ILL.; Celus Fasteners Mfg., Inc., Andover, MA.; Crawford Products, Inc., West Hanover, MA.; Devcon Consumer Products, Detroit, MI.; G.P. Foster, Cordage Institute, Hingham, MA.; David M. Groff, Wallpapering Instructional Resources, Kingston, N.C.; Hillwood Manufacturing Company, Cleveland, OH.; Keystone Steel and Wire, Peoria, ILL.; Master Appliance, Racine, WI.; National Forest Products Association, Washington, D.C.; National Paint and Coatings Association, Washington, D.C.; Pan American Screw, Hickory, N.C.; Red Devil, Inc., Union, N.J.; Robertson Whitehouse, Toronto, Ont.; Ryobi Canada Inc., Cambridge, Ont.; The Schundler Company, Metuchen, N.J.; Thomas D. Searles, American Lumber Standards Committee, Germantown, MD.; Security Fastener Co., Benicia, CA.; Sharon Fastener Company, Solon, OH.; Skil Corporation, Chicago, ILL.; Themans, Inc., Virginia Beach, VA.; Ungar Division of Eldon Industries, Subsidiary of Rubbermaid Corp., Buena Park, CA.; Wall Industries, Inc. Granite Quarry, N.C.

The following persons also assisted in the preparation of this book:

Graphor Consultation, Maryse Doray, Shirley Grynspan, Francine Lemieux, Jennifer Meltzer, Robert Paquet, Maryo Proulx, Shirley Sylvain